I0119652

Anonymous

Anglia Rediviva

No defence of the aristocratic party, but of the king and people, mutually

restored to their constitutional action

Anonymous

Anglia Rediviva
No defence of the aristocratic party, but of the king and people, mutually restored to their constitutional action

ISBN/EAN: 9783337064716

Printed in Europe, USA, Canada, Australia, Japan

Cover: Foto ©Suzi / pixelio.de

More available books at **www.hansebooks.com**

ANGLIA REDIVIVA:

NO DEFENCE OF THE

ARISTOCRATIC PARTY,

BUT OF THE

KING AND PEOPLE,

MUTUALLY RESTORED TO

THEIR CONSTITUTIONAL ACTION,

WITH

THE COUNTRY AT LARGE TO IT's DIGNITY,

AND THE

BLESSINGS OF IT's FREE GOVERNMENT,

BY A REFORM IN THE

REPRESENTATION AND DURATION

OF

PARLIAMENT.

——————— NOTHING EXTENUATE,
NOR SET DOWN AUGHT IN MALICE.

Shakefpeare's Othello.

LONDON,

Printed: and fold by T. CADELL, in the STRAND.

CONTENTS.

CHAP. I.

CHAP. II.

ſtitution; this act diſcuſſed—boroughs hardly more deſenſible, but for their antiquity—a glorious patriotiſm in thoſe that can give them up.

C H A P. III.

The PERNICIOUS CONSEQUENCES *of an unequal Re-preſentation, in the nature of things.*

Repreſentatives of ſmall local intereſts never think of being accountable—ſuch are conſtant materials for Miniſters to work with—a ſingular apology for Boroughs an-ſwered—the danger of an unequal Repreſentation illu-ſtrated in a ſtriking inſtance—others more to be dreaded equally poſſible.

C H A P. IV.

Firſt Advantage that will reſult from a reformed Repre-ſentation: ARISTOCRATIC PARTY *annihilated.*

The unnatural and diſproportionate graſp of Power by the Nobility—but moſt inordinate in thoſe who feel the ſpirit of Ariſtocratic connections—both to the ſovereign autho-rity—and alſo to the People—the views of Ariſtocracy favored by an unequal Repreſentation; by Boroughs—more compleatly aſſiſted by the Statute 8 Hen. VI. *by which Counties became but larger Boroughs—property the foundation and genius of Ariſtocracy—Similitude be-*

tween

tween the Ariſtocratic regulation of Election *by* Servius Tullus *and the ſtatute* 8 Henry VI.—*Ariſtocracy by theſe means knit into a* Faction—*and uniform in the means of preſerving it's power—as profeſſing patriotic principles, theſe bounded by an oppoſition to royal prerogative—the* Patriotiſm *expected by the People broader and more radical than this—the People conſtantly deſerted by the Ariſtocratic Party on conſtitutional points—a tribute of reſpect to the private virtues of many* who *compoſe that Party—how a reform of the* Repreſentation *will naturally annihilate it—ſuch a* Faction *annihilated, every branch of character will feel a new Being—the Man of Abilities—the* Miniſter—*the* Crown—*the* Country *at large—anſwer to part of a late Speech at* Weſtminſter—*and to ſimilar matter in a Pamphlet, entitled,* Thoughts on Diſcontents.

C H A P. V.

Second Advantage *that will reſult from a reformed Repreſentation:* THE CROWN *reſtored to its conſtitutional Action.*

The due Prerogatives of the Crown to be valued and *cheriſhed — the ſpecific importance of the regal power —this underwent* a *revolution in* 1688—*Independence, the great original principle of the regal power— this evidenced by great antiquity in it's controul over the Parliamentary branches—in it's controul over the orders of Subject's by* Rights *yet ſubſiſting—but eſpecially in the royal demeſnes, the original* proviſion *for the Crown—much dependance introduced by a Civil-Liſt-Support—Advantage taken* of the Crown under *this change by Party —the*

—the influence of Party on the executive Power, in it's whole operations—in appointment to the offices of State—hence the influence of a Miniſtry ſubſtituted for that of the Crown, in the enforcement of it's own meaſures—how far the ſpirit of true Whigiſm is concerned in theſe effects—high time that the true friends of the Conſtitution ſhould be diſtinguiſhed from Republican Whigs—The application: A reform of Parliamentary Repreſentation the natural cure of theſe wrongs—Independency reſtored to one Eſtate muſt be followed by independency to another, or there is no balance—the royal negative muſt conſequently feel itſelf in force—an Addreſs to the Crown.

C H A P. VI.

The DURATION of Parliament:

Intimately connected with the ſubject of Repreſentation—the greatneſs of delegated power ſhould ever be balanced by it's brevity of duration—by the wiſdom of moſt States the period of a year has been adopted—this the ancient policy of our own Country in the parliamentary Truſt—how it came to be varied—partly by the acquieſcence of the People in triennial acts—the ſeptennial act the groſſeſt violation of Law, Conſtitution, and Decency—that act muſt at all events be done away—how much farther we muſt go—without ſhort Parliaments no amendment of the Repreſentation can do good.

O R,

ENGLAND RESTORED, &c.

CHAP. I.

The Constitution of England a subject of constant admiration—
a jealousy for it natural in Englishmen—the Rights of the
People, which form the House of Commons, original and
unperishable—the Constitution not to be taken from the
Revolution in 1688, which left abuses—Constitutional
Principles naturally call for occasional adjustment—within
certain limits, each constituent part of the State has a full
right to call for modifications—Application to the subject
of Parliamentary Representation—the History of the House
of Commons for the last fourteen years; which gives impa-
tience to the call for reform—but at any rate makes a candid
discussion and enquiry indispensible—happy for England,
the time now favorable to this; and the Minister.

THE Constitution of the English Government has
been a subject of great admiration in every age,
not only with those who were born to the enjoyment of it,
and therefore may be deemed naturally partial to their
own inheritance, but with all enlightened and observing
Foreigners, whose distance enables them to view this
illustrious work of Art in a calmer and more sober
light, unaffected by the glare of colouring. Unques-

B   tionably

tionably no nation in the world hath shared a government, built on monarchic principles, equally genial in it's spirit, and compleat in it's model; though it be similar in many of it's first principles to what other countries have sometime enjoyed, as it flowed from the same fountain which directed it's streams to other parts, but it has been more happy than all others in the preservation and improvement of what it has received. By the adversity of genius, or of local circumstances, neighboring countries have seen these genial seeds of national happiness and freedom wither in their hands, or choaked before they came to maturity of growth. To the soil, and the air, of Britain it seems to have been reserved to rear the precious plant into perfection: while the genius of her People appears no less singularly turned to the very nice and delicate culture of so rare a possession.

A jealousy for it natural in Englishmen.

From the national character of Britons may therefore be expected a peculiar jealousy for the Constitution, which seems possible to have been maintained by no other care than their own. There was once a people in the world, with whom it was an established law of their state, that every man, from the moment he came to rational life, should give proofs of his acquaintance with the constitutional government of his country, and of his zeal to maintain it. If any people under heaven could ever be bribed by the importance of their interests, to become Politicians through all their classes, the temptation most certainly rests with Englishmen; and especially those who have lived in the most advantageous period of the Constitution, as it has been considerably secured in the last hundred years; but those more especially still, who now live to see how near they have lately been brought to the loss of this inestimable Constitution, (nor yet are they

secured

fecured from the fear) by an Adminiftration inimical to it's principles, and rendered undaunted in their fyftem by the long tenure of their power.

The Frame of Government, under which we live, muft be allowed to have advanced progreffively to it's prefent ftate. The Houfe of Commons in particular, which forms the feat of popular intereft, and the great check which the people have referved to themfelves in the Govern-ment, has rifen in fucceffive periods not only to the prefent modification of it's power, but to that power itfelf. Yet the whole that it poffeffes was not only it's due in the nature of things, but inherent in the firft principles of it's own inftitution. In like manner, thofe popular rights, which give the very formation to the Houfe of Commons, whatever variations either in form or in effect they may have received from the influence of time and the mutability of things, muft ftill remain immutable in their fpirit, and inextinguifhable in their claim, nay and indifpenfible in their prefervation, as the pillar on which the whole fuperftructure refts. So that it is of no moment in the mouth of an objector, *when* any one of thofe rights firft affumed any one fhape it may have taken, or *when* it loft that fhape for another: Neither will the reafoning be always juft, which would affume the accidental form of any popular right for the full force of that right itfelf, and argue from the habits, which have found their way into matters of conftitutional procedure, to the exiftence of the Conftitution itfelf in it's true and genuin deftination.

The Rights of the People, which form the Houfe of Com-mons, original and unperifh-able.

W

The Constitution not to be taken from the Revolution in 1688, which left abuses.

We have juſt obſerved, that the Revolution in 1688 was a moſt advantageous period for the Conſtitution. But this muſt be underſtood with limitation. The Conſtitution was then ſecured, but in partial, though momentous, circumſtances. Theſe more immediately related to the prerogative of the Crown, and thoſe Rights of the People, in which the ſecurity of their perſons and property was veſted. The convulſions, which preceded that event, ſprung out of theſe ſubjeĉts, and therefore found their cure in the proviſions eſtabliſhed by *the Declaration of Rights*. But there were abuſes, or at leaſt deviations from conſtitutional Purity, and theſe in points of the firſt magnitude, which had been growing with time ; theſe were loſt in the more clamorous grievances, which then preſſed upon men's minds, and therefore they found no part in the remedies of the age. I allude here to thoſe fundamental Rights of the People, by which they form their own Houſe of Repreſentatives, and give it every quality that moſt naturally may belong to a repreſentative body. So that we are not to look upon the Revolution as a full eſtabliſhment of the Conſtitution, or to conſider any exerciſe of the Crown, or of the People drawn into it by habit, or of the repreſentative body tempted to it by the ſweets of power, as concluſively definitive of right, more eſpecially if it was not then the ſubject of an expreſs proviſional adjuſtment.

Conſtitutional Principles naturally call for occaſional adjuſtment.

The only correĉt view we can therefore have of our political rights is, by looking to what the Conſtitution *is*, rather than to what it may *ſeem* to be by the prevalence of accidental habits. And thoſe principles, which form the great outlines of it, as they are perennial in their nature, ſo they evermore call for occaſional adjuſtment, whenever the departure from their ſpirit ſhall
                                                                    threaten

threaten the lofs of their effect. If the original frame
of Government be worth preferving, this is unqueftionably both juft and wife. The alternative is fhort and
plain : Either you muft refit the Pillars, efpecially when
encreafing decays go faft to undermine, or the fabric
will crumble : either the land-marks muft maintain their
place, and alfo be kept up to fight, or the property
will be loft. Mr. *Locke*, in his chapter *on the Diffolution
of Government*, has clearly proved, that when the firft
principles of it are broken through and fubverted, the
People, who are the great Fountain of Power, and the
primary objefts for whofe good all Government is or
ought to be formed, may take the matter into their
own hands, and new-model it in a way, by which they
conceive the original purpofes of their freedom and
happinefs may be better maintained. If there be, as I
fhould think, fcarcely an individual in thefe enlightened
days, when the ideas of Government, it's origin, and
it's end are more liberally conceived, who would referve
his acknowledgment of this doftrine ; it feems however
hardly poffibly to fuppofe that plain fenfe or a liberal
apprehenfion can hefitate on another point, which is
circumfcribed by a much narrower extent—that when
any primary Rights of the People, though far from being
annihilated, become fo defaced and mutilated in their
exercife, that the change introduced tends faft to put
the right itfelf out of fight, and to extinguifh the objeft
of it, there can be no controul on their claim to new-
model the exercife, fo as to make it more produftive of
it's end, nor ought there to be any refiftance to their
voice.

This matter, important as it is, must strike us forcibly on the first blush of it, but with increasing conviction on every investigation. It has it's boundaries, and while they are plain, they give greater energy to the principle they encircle. In the distributions of Government, the powers allotted to each constituent part are sacred. The people, though the fountain of all, having made this distribution, have given from themselves those estates, which they can never more invade, so as to unsettle, unless the common bond of all be dissolved by the fault of the others. They cannot even move the line which encircles their own estate; for in this case, to move is to trespass. But within these boundaries, and especially within their own, they can act more free. Whatever relates to the mere modification of their own check upon the other estates, they can from time to time revise, correct, and amend; they can repair it's defects, renovate it's decays, supply what has lapsed by time, reduce or lop off what by time has become inconveniently exuberant, so as to prove a dead weight on the important function. And more especially are these acts right and fit, where the intention is not to introduce new modes, but to give revived vigour to those, which are stamped with the sanction of past and early ages. For in any of these cases, there is no line of separation disturbed, no barrier is removed, no other interest is affected, but in such way as it should desire to be affected, by seeing the fence between itself and another properly maintained, for the common preservation of order and advantage to each. For the line, which runs between these respective estates, is actually a fence and a barrier to each, which no longer answers it's purpose, or very little longer, than it is kept straight and strong. If the internal works on either side, which are designed to buttress and make

it a wall of mutual effective refiftance, are fuffered to
relax, to lofe their hold, and fall into decay, it will
prefently lean from the fuperior preffure on the other
fide; and the time will be fhort, before it will be laid
level with the ground; expofing the whole domain,
which was fo negligently fecured, to all the confequences
of a defperate irruption from more potent interefts,
whofe lofs of their own compact fituation may, moft
likely, in the general confufion prove fatal to themfelves. It is therefore for the good of all, as well as
of any feparate eftate, that the barriers of each fhould
be kept up in their natural ftrength by conftant reno-
vations. If thefe are called for within another eftate than
their own, the People, for whofe benefit the whole
is contrived, have an unqueftionable right of interference: But it is fufficient for my prefent defign, that
their power of correction is paramount all controul
within their own. And if, for the fake of order, the
concurrence of the other eftates be regularly needful
here, yet the Voice of the People calling for that concurrence, and much more calling to thofe whom they
have deputed to fpeak and act for themfelves, fhould
never meet any poffible refiftance: if it does, from any
quarter whatfoever, either all Government is an impo-
fition on common fenfe, and worfe than none, or the
moment is arrived when regularity muft give way to
felf-prefervation, and they may take up fome better
means of giving themfelves juftice, and burfting through
the fhackles that would tie their hands from warding
off the ruin, whofe precipitate ftrides are haftening
before their eyes,

The

The obfervations, which have been hitherto employed, have had an immediate view to the right and importance of reftoring to priftine virtue and extent that great and comprehenfive groundwork of the People's weight and fecurity, THEIR REPRESENTATION IN PARLIAMENT; which gives the effence to the Houfe of Commons, forms the popular check or balance in the State, and according as it is naturally and with confiderable equality preferved, or as it lofes it's fpring from the general mafs of the people, becomes the fource of every evil which can be conceived to flow to a nation, whofe Lives, Liberties and Property are at the mercy of an Affembly, over which it has no regular, compleat, and exclufive hold. If there be a fubject in the whole affemblage of national Rights, which in the nature of the cafe may moft naturally be expected to call for revifion and reform, it is unqueftionably this before us. When for a long fucceffion of time the Reprefentation of a Country has been occupied, fo very confiderably as our's is, by the fuffrages of more private and local fituations, inftead of the more general and diffufed interefts of counties; what can be more looked for, than that towns and boroughs, depending perhaps for their welfare on the accidental circumftances of trade or fituation, may participate in the eternal mutability of things, and vary their condition with the varying courfe of human affairs? And in this cafe, what confequence *fhould* follow, but that having changed their condition, their firft proportion of reprefentation fhould no longer be their due? If their condition be changed for the worfe, then the humble cottage, or the whole tenantry of the lonely village, can never deferve that weight in the National Scale, which is denied to the expanded wealth and commercial greatnefs of the neigh-

boring town, that hath legitimately eclipfed the prof-
perity of the other. If for the better, then if the
principle was right, by which they firft gained a meafure
of Reprefentation, not only that meafure fhould follow
them in their rife, but fhould become the acquifition of
thofe other rifing Communities, which had never gained
it at all. Thus we fee, that conftituted as the Reprefentation is, it generates eternal difficulties; if we
meant to give it any femblance of rational Reform, we
fhould never be at a certainty for an age together:
indeed the calls for Reform would never ceafe: And the
truth is, that they never can, let what meliorations foever
be beftowed, till the national Reprefentation be put on
that extended bafis, which will make it the genuin off-
fpring of the whole People, and fo give it ftability for
ever.

If the nature of the cafe be a ftanding call for Reform,
the alarms, into which the want of that Reform hath
brought us within the laft fourteen years particularly,
muft add impatience to the demand. To enumerate
what *England* has fuffered, in all her deareft circumftances,
within that period from a Houfe of Commons, which
having not even the form of reprefenting her aright, but
unhappily the form, without the virtue, of a third eftate
concurring to public acts, hath bound her to what an age
of conftitutional exertions and the pureft public œconomy
hardly can recover; this will be a tafk for the diffufe
hiftoric page. My purpofe muft fkim more lightly over
the furface. Other æras have feen this reprefentative
body too much devoted to the Minifters of the Crown;
but it was referved for the period I have mentioned to
compleat it's full difgrace, and to fhew us by real facts,
rifing in ignominious and ruinous progreffion, what a

The hiftory the Houfe Commons f the laft fou teen years; which gives impatience t the call for Reform.

C   fenfible

sensible foreigner foresaw and foretold*, " that the " liberties of *Britain* were near their fall, when the " Legislative Body should become as corrupt as the " executive, and dependent thereon."

By wretched notions of Politics, fostered by men who were conscious to themselves either of a want of virtue in their plans, or of inability to govern by more plain and manly means, they had for some time been maturing the system of bringing the Legislative Body to be the right arm of the executive power. It were obvious, that if once the former could be made pliant to the will of the Minister, every extension of the prerogative he might desire, every daring measure to spread the influence of the Crown, might not only be obtained, but, in case of discontent, be safe in it's exercise behind the screen of those legal forms, which had given it birth, and whose act it therefore became.

An heathen poet † has observed, that *no man ever reached the height of wickedness at first*: But the Minister of that day in the House of Commons boldly gave the lie to the general feelings of the human breast, and renounced for himself the credit, which that universally approved aphorism gave to the backwardness of virtue in evacuating the heart. It is perhaps from the abyss of political depravity that nature withdraws her feelings and her rules, as unable to find their subsistence there ; so that the most perfect amiableness of the private man cannot survive in the breast of the Minister. One of the earliest efforts, by which that baneful system gave an earnest of it's own views, and of the subserviency of the

---

* Montesquieu. † Juvenal.

Commons, went to an extent of invafion on the Rights of the People, which fapped the foundation of them at once, left the people nothing to enjoy with confidence, and fubftituted a medium for making their Reprefentatives no longer a check upon the executive branch. What confequences lefs direful to all the purpofes intended to be fecured by a third eftate of the People, can we fuppofe to follow, when thofe Reprefentatives, creating difabilities by their own vote, and annexing to that vote the force and fanction of compleat law, deny to their Conftituents the power of chufing the men, whom they may think fit to fend with their own truft into the delegated body? Having with fuch temerity infringed the facred choice of their Electors, we cannot wonder to fee them, at another moment, gratify the moft profufe expenditure of public money, by making good a large arrear, which in any reafonable view could never have been incurred for a good or an excufable purpofe; while at the fame time they covered the corruption which they fed, by refufing to enquire or know how that expenditure had arifen. A feries of feffions paffes on, replete with the proofs of the moft abfolute and aftonifhing fervility to the will of the Minifter in every circumftance of their truft.—If the interefts of the people are formidably threatned in any part of the empire by the apparent mifconduct of Adminiftration; not a fingle paper will thefe Truftees of thofe interefts confent to be produced for the difcovery of truth:—If the Liberties of the People are threatned, in circumftances of the deareft importance, by the perverfions of law either in courts of juftice, or in law-officers of the Crown; not the leaft inquiry that may correct the abufe, and relieve generations to come from oppreffion, will thefe Guardians of thofe liberties permit:—If it affifts the views of

C 2

an Administration hostile to freedom, to try the precedent of an arbitrary form of Government, by beginning with a distant part of the British Dominions; though by that Establishment one fundamental Pillar of the Constitution, supporting expressly the utmost extent of British Dominions that ever should accrue, THE ACT OF UNIFORMITY, was most palpably overturned: This venal Assembly makes no hesitation, but establishes in *Canada* a system which may overleap even the daring and malevolent extension of her new bounds, and defy the Atlantic herself to bar it's triumph over all that British generations have enjoyed and loved:—If prerogative desires to enlarge itself at home, though possibly, and not improbably, to the subversion of another fundamental Pillar of the State, THE ACT OF SETTLEMENT; the controul over the marriages of the Royal Family may pass with unobserving minds for a private and limited concern, and accordingly this pliant body surrenders up along with these individuals the eventual succession of the Crown to the royal arbitrement:— Amidst these things, we are shocked to see, in profound peace, an establishment of expence not only more enormous than ever was known, but growing immensely every year, granted by these stewards of the public purse in the gross, and without account, as in the gross it was required;—granted with an inattention, which shews, if possible, more shamefully than the extent of their profusion, the servility and forgetfulness of duty to which they were arrived; for while millions of their Constituents money were passing away, you would have imagined it an Assembly brought together for idle chit-chat, or tumultuous dissipation. So extreme, in short, was the controul of the Minister over the Commons in this period, that public virtue, or however

virtuous

virtuous hope, feemed to be fickened in the honeft few; who, after ftruggling all they could to refift the betrayers of their country, while a dead calm of things promifed no events which might break the evil concert of the Executive Cabinet, began to think of retreating from fcenes, which they could neither endure nor prevent, as the only refuge that was left them.

But a period next opens, at the mention of which the ears of every Englifhman will tingle to the lateft generations. A Houfe of Commons, which had given fuch pledges of it's compleat fubmiffivenefs, might reafonably be counted ripe for any meafures of thofe, who would ftick at none for the ftrengthening of their fyftem. Indeed there remained but few branches of power, on which attempts had not been made, and with much fuccefs, to gather fomething which might form a part of Minifterial Influence; nor any mean of corruption within the Realm, which had not been put to the ftretch. And yet the demands of corruption encreafed with the gratifications it yielded. The Dependents of the corrupted formed a numerous train no lefs to be fatiated, where all things are to be bought, than the principals themfelves. But *England* was heavy-laden, and *Ireland* could not bear another pound in addition to her weight. *America* was light and free: In the various Governments of her extended Continent there would be ample room for all that a corrupting Minifter could wifh, if once they could be brought within the grafp of Parliament for revenue: From her fruitful and unbroken foil would then arife a harveft, in which a whole Nation of Expectants might fill their bofoms with the fheaves. The feed was fown: It took root: It grew: The harveft was near: But then the owners ftrongly forbad the ftranger's foot to enter, or his hand to reap. To covet is hostility commenced: When once the heart is possessed by the passion, the hand will soon make the deed it's own. An intolerant Ministry draws the sword, which haply the setting sun of Britain shall only see returned into it's sheath.

But what if Ministry draws the sword? The People of *England*, looking not through the same medium with Ministry, but feeling sensibly the benefits of amity with their Transatlantic Brethren, in their Commerce, their Lands, in every circumstance which formed their astonishing prosperity, fain would have suspended the arm uplifted to desolation. It is a justice to their integrity and good sense, that no measure could ever come forth more universally unpopular than this American War. The voice of the Nation, from one end to the other, rung in exclamation against it. They spoke most feelingly to the Throne; they spoke to the Legislature, where any opening of occasion was given them to speak. If contentment, if acquiescence in what struck at the received ideas of national interest, kindred affection, and honorable justice, was heard in any quarter, it was but from those who manufactured the weapons, that were to deluge *America* with blood.*

Let us now see how the voice of those, with whom it rested to speak the public sense in Parliament, corresponded with the duty they owed their Constituents. Deaf, insensible, impenetrable to the wishes of a whole Nation, they boldly enter the lists at the Minister's call, and run the race which he sets before them. The People were of opinion that the Americans were aggrieved and injured:—But these Representatives pronounce them rebellious;

* Address from *Birmingham*.

rebellious; vote bills to starve one part of them to death, to cancel all the established Rights and Securities of another, and to encourage the Military in going all lengths to keep down the spirit that might speak it's oppressions. The People feel the wonted resources of their Commerce, diffusing itself through an infinity of channels, to be affected: These **Representatives** shut up every port, and put a stop at once to every means of American intercourse. The former, naturally alarmed for themselves, beg to be heard; and their petitions, by an insidious artifice, are consigned to *a committee of oblivion.* The *Americans* offer a golden bridge—they offer to accept an alternative of dependence, only wishing to shun the condition of direct slavery, to which no alternative is given: The People of *England* are anxious that this favourable moment should be embraced, and the formidable breach thus passed in time; but their Representatives, with the other branches of the Legislature, will have no bridge, they will fight it in the deep. The People bending under their public debt, and feeling all private property reduced by the loss of that commercial influx, which gave a lift to all their circumstances, sink in despondency under the additional burdens of so distant and complicated a War: Their Representatives become Egyptian task-masters; they will have, notwithstanding, *the tale of bricks,* let *the straw* be found where it may.

Here indeed the scene opens anew. To what extent soever the Minister's imagination might have carried the accession of Ministerial influence in case of final success; enough to satisfy even an unreasonable mind now arose, in the mean time, from the enormous grants of Parliament, to keep that Parliament, and other numerous dependants, at his beck. In reviewing these

unparalleled

unparalleled profusions, they become in some sort fabulous
to the mind that has marked the usual capacities of
national wealth ;—all *Europe* might well stand aghast at
them ; yet no imagination of others can exceed the
painful feelings entailed upon those that are doomed to
bear them. The *English* Nation, because the Mart of
Nations, is indeed a *Phænomenon* of Wealth : Her Wars
for some time have been an *Unique* of Expenditure, at
least to *European* experience : But all that have passed
before this that I am speaking of, if looked at by the
measure of Expenditure exhibited in this, might seem
more fitly the short and puny conflicts of some most
petty State, than the hard-fought Wars of *England*,
coping with the first Powers in the World. Let her
own Expenditures therefore give the measure of com-
parison, of which we shall set before the Reader a
Sketch, as it will be useful to shew these Representatives
of the People in their genuin character.

On the head of GENERAL SUPPLY, the whole may
come out at one view ;—that from the commencement
of this War to the present year, being the seventh, and
including forty Millions, which are known to be yet
unfunded, and a large unliquidated Debt in America,
no less than 140 Millions have been expended—a Sum
more than seventeen Millions beyond what the Nation
had incurred as a Debt from the first existence of it's Funds
in the Reign of King *William* to the commencement of
the present War ; though near a century has passed, and
in that space of time full six-and-thirty years have been
consumed by *England* in her wars, previous to the
present.

The

The following are but fubordinate to this aftonifhing aggregate of Expence, but they are worth attention for the part they fhare in it.—On the head of ARMY EXTRAORDINARIES—that moft horrid fource of Corruption, becaufe they are not only incurred, but paid, by the Minifter himfelf, without difcretion left to Parliament—it has appeared, from the public accounts, that thefe in any ONE year of the prefent War fall fhort, on an average, but little more than 100,000*l.* of the Extraordinaries for THE WHOLE of TWO GREAT WARS, which lafted TWENTY years.

Again: In ONE year of the prefent war, thefe amount, within half a Million, to the WHOLE SUPPLY of one year in *Queen Ann's* war.

Again: In the FOUR firft years of the prefent War, thefe *exceed* by 4,640,449 *l.* all the Extraordinaries of the FOUR firft years of the laft War.

Take one view more. In any FOUR years of the prefent War, thefe amount to *a Million and a half Sterling* more than all the Extraordinaries of Wars which took up *nine-and-twenty* years, from King *William's* time to the laft War of *George the Second.*

On the head of NAVY EXTRAORDINARIES—after rifing regularly above a Million every year fince this War began, thefe now *exceed* the Extraordinaries in the *higheft* year of the laft War, by confiderably more than *two Millions* of Money.

On the head of ORDNANCE—it appears, that the Eftimate for ONE year in this War comes within fo fmall

D   a fum

a fum as 100,000*l.* of what was expended in THREE years
from 1745, with a Rebellion in the Country, which
called for extraordinary ammunition, &c. It approaches
within the inconfiderable fum of 79,000*l.* to what was
the expence of the THREE firft years of the laft war;
and within the trifling difference of 5000*l.* to the TWO
next years of that War, which were ftill higher eftimated:
And it *exceeds* by near half a Million the higheft
year of all.

Thus have the People been loaded by a Houfe of
Commons fervile to thofe on whofe meafures they
fhould have been a check, and falfe to thofe from whom
they derived their truft. But if thefe *Facts* demonftrate,
to our coft, their entire fubferviency to the will of the
Minifter, a proof remains behind, which will fhew this yet
more to their fhame, if it be poffible. If there be a
circumftance, which marks, beyond every other, a mind
wedded to corruption, hardened in flagitioufnefs, and
incurably bafe, it is when men are brought, by a train
of evil confequences, to fee the pernicioufnefs of their
own meafures, and to condemn them, and yet remain
unconverted from the evil principle: In other words,
when we ftill adhere to the deceiver, and court his
continued deception, while he owns without referve
that he has feduced and betrayed us. Into this dif-
graceful predicament, to this *damning* proof of their
hardened corruption, were thefe Reprefentatives of the
People brought. By the adverfe chance of war, the
Minifter was obliged to fhift his ground, and to turn
round upon his own principles. He drops the haughty
tone he had held: He decries the expectations he himfelf had raifed: He acknowledges himfelf miftaken:
He declares that he muft look no longer for that, to

obtain

abtain which he had beguiled Parliament to draw the
fword. What do the Commons, hearing this language
fo difaftrous to thofe, who had fold their own character
and the interefts of their Country to the ambition of
him, who thus chilled every feeling within them ? What
would *honeft*, what would *miftaken*, men have done here ?
We muft change the terms of our queftion, or the event
will never be guefled at. What would *corrupt* men
have done ? Exactly what thefe did. They clung to
the corruption. With more than feminine infatuation
they hung on the man that had undone them. They
turned round with him to his own language : They
condemned with him the policy they had purfued ;
yet they abode, with him, in the policy they condemned. They joined in confeffing the miferies,
which had flowed from their meafures ; yet their
Country profited nothing from their conviction. Dan-
gers and misfortunes, which make other minds ferious,
could not turn their's to the part where their duty
refted. They were the Minifter's flaves in his errors,
as well as in his firft delufions.

If it be poffible for the people of *England* to bear,
without correction, fuch demonftrations as thefe of
perfidioufnefs in their own Delegates : if it be poffible
for them to fuffer their Houfe of Commons to continue
fo abfurdly conftituted, as with fuch facility to generate
this oblivioufnefs of what they owe to their conftituents :
then is not only all public virtue fled from fociety, but
all private fenfe of felf-prefervation.

Building on thefe foundations the neceffity of that
Reform in the Houfe of Commons, to which the views
of public men have for fome time been involuntarily

directed

directed by the continued abufes, of which I have given but an imperfect fketch ; I have no fcruple in pronouncing, that from the want of a more equal reprefentation of the people, and a fhorter duration to the Parliamentary truft, all thofe abufes have arifen, and that by a Reform in thefe circumftances they will all be cured, and prevented at leaft from becoming fo formidable in future. At any rate, the reafoning and the facts, which, I conceive, I have incontrovertibly employed, muft operate, I fhould hope, on every candid and honeft mind fo far as to give this fubject a claim to be heard and comprehenfively difcuffed in the place, from whence the Reform muft regularly proceed. If the difcuffion terminates even in a confiderable extent of the Reform, though it be dear and irkfome to buy again what we ought never to have loft, yet the evils we have endured from the abufes will be cheaply laid out in the purchafe of what will enrich us fo much : we will almoft confent to kifs the rod, which in fcourging us hath been followed by fo great a good. So it happens often, by a Providential Difpofal, that the extremeft evils become their own cure ; and Nations, like Individuals, find unaccountably their happieft fortune to fpring from what covered them, in the moments of action, with defpondency, and feemed the inevitable crufh of fate.

I flatter myfelf therefore, that the Title, which I have given to thefe Sheets, though large in it's pretenfions, is by no means unfitly applied to the Reform, which is the object of my writing, nor will be found in the iffue more fanguine than the falutary effects of that Reform will juftify. With refpect to the attainment of it, there is a moment now before us, which may fairly bid our hopes be ftrong. *England* now, for the firft time in all

her

Margin notes: at any makes a d difcufnd inquiry penfible. — pyfor Engl, the time favorable this ; and Minifter.

her Hiftory, fees a Prime-Minifter cordially pledged to the recovery of a more *free* and more *equal* Reprefentation of the People, and *by that means*, as well as every other, to the rendering of the Houfe of Commons more independent of the executive branch, by as much as it fhall become more dependent on it's own fource, the People at large. Heaven forbid! that we fhould look with coolnefs on thofe other checks upon corruption, to which the integrity of other Minifters, or other public characters, hath rifen ; or that we fhould bereave them of their deferved meafure of applaufe. But in the objects I am fpeaking of unqueftionably refts the moft unqualified proof of friendfhip to the People ; and the Minifter, who will devote to the eftablifhment of thofe objects the weight that naturally attends on his fituation, can have no competitor for the Patriot-Character : becaufe he demonftrates his love for the Conftitution ; fuperior to all partial intervening interefts, he feeks to reftore the proper check of the People in the Government to it's natural tone ; and in bracing that check, he braces thofe others that are framed into it, and form the compact workmanfhip which holds all together ;—he lays the axe to the root of corrupt and pernicious influence, not only that which arifes from the luxuriant diforders of the natural branches, but much more that which is felt from thofe unnatural excrefcences, which are no part of the tree itfelf, but cleave to it as a poifonous *fungus*, which not only disfigures it's beauty, but debilitates the health of both root and branch. Let him give the Country thefe renovated Rights, and this new vigour in her Government, and let him not fear that the man who fo honorably throws himfelf on the power of the Country will want the firm fupport of a grateful and difcerning People ; his power may add to its ordinary

compafs

compaſs the ſure poſſeſſion of their hearts: They will never fear the abilities, which ſhall have given ſuch proofs of their kind and genial influence: and preſently we ſhall ſee the mutual intereſts of Prince and People, forgetting jealouſy and complaint on either ſide move in an harmonious alliance, which will be both the ſtronger, when each poſſeſſes an independance of it's own, and the cloſer alſo, when that independance is yet ſo reſpectively involved, that the one maintains the other in it's place.

This will prepare us to ſtate the ſubject of REPRESENTATION—it's groſs *defects*—the *pernicious conſequences* which unavoidably flow from thoſe defects—the *comprehenſive advantages* which will accrue from giving them a conſtitutional Correction. Having diſcuſſed theſe points, I ſhall ſpeak to another matter, which though often conſidered as a diſtinct inquiry, yet ſtrictly, makes a part of the great ſubject of REPRESENTATION, and, as now conſtituted, has it's full ſhare in all the political evils of which we can complain; I mean the DURATION of Parliament.

CHAP.

CHAP. II.

A juſt Representation briefly ſtated—the groſs defects and inequality of ours in the Electors—in the Elected—this branch of the Conſtitution quite defunct—an anſwer to the argument againſt Reform, that the Conſtitution has ſtood hitherto—neither Law nor Habits neceſſarily make the Conſtitution—the 8 Hen. 6. a breach of the Conſtitution; this act diſcuſſed—boroughs hardly more defenſible, but for their antiquity—a glorious patriotiſm in thoſe that can give them up.

A Man of ſimple capacity will come with little reflexion to that idea of popular Repreſentation, A juſt Repreſentation briefly ſtated. which muſt be juſt in the nature of things, and is confirmed by the pureſt times of thoſe countries that enjoy it. That idea common ſenſe as well as common law hath expreſſed by this general rule, *that he who bears the burden ought to enjoy the benefit.* In no poſſible circumſtances can theſe terms be applied with more pointed energy, than to the caſe before us. The *burden,* to which we ſtand here, may be the loſs of all that is dear to men : To have a voice therefore in guarding that burden muſt be the deareſt *benefit.* I do not ſay that there are no exceptions to this rule. In every civil privilege whatever, wiſdom hath made an exception of thoſe private circumſtances, which tend to deſtroy all the public good of the privilege itſelf. Now that public good is endangered by thoſe circumſtances of an individual, which leave him not properly capable or free to judge and act in this important function. Inexperience of years, below the received age of manhood—indigence of condition, which contributes nothing to the public aſſiſtance.

affiftance, and much more, if it fubfifts at all by that affiftance—fervitude, which is fubject to influences that fuffer it not to follow it's own will—thefe are evermore reafonable difabilities, which give a line of confinement to the right. But within thefe boundaries, there feems little to be faid on other limitations, if we would have the right in it's purity: And candour will hardly urge confiderations of *expediency*, any more than reafon will find them fufficient, to overturn what may be claimed as a *birth-right* in every State that has a pretence to be free. The man who is worth no land, the man who is worth no money, the man who has nothing but the bread he eats from his induftry, has his life and the fruits of that induftry at ftake, which may be as much aggrieved by thofe that make laws, as the lives and properties of thofe that are greater and richer than himfelf; and the State is not free, which does not give every man, feeling himfelf free in mind and condition, a power of guarding what is thus dear to all.

The grofs de- Looking on the Parliamentary Reprefentation of
fects and ine- Englifhmen in this fcale, we are confounded in a moment
quality of ours; with it's aftonifhing departure from what carries the
femblance of Proportion, Reafon, and Common Senfe.
The view of this matter is two-fold, in both of which we
fhall ftate it—the Right of Suffrage—and the Members
Elected; in other words, the People reprefented—and
the Members reprefenting.

In the Electors With refpect to the firft: The number of inhabitants
in *England* and *Wales* is computed to be about *five
millions*. Of thefe, were the Right of Suffrage reformed
on the fcale above-mentioned, it is fuppofed by the moft
accurate invefligations, that about *twelve hundred thoufand*
would

would be capable of voting: Whereas, at prefent, little more than *two hundred thoufand* do vote. So that it is only *one* out of *fix* that enjoys the common Birthright.

If we view this Difproportion, as it operates through the country, we fhall find it ftill more irregular in it's diftribution. Out of the whole number that vote, nearly *two-thirds*, or 130,000 Suffrages, are employed in the election of only a *fixth part* of the Houfe of Commons, or 92 Members for the Counties. Here the Proportion is of 1413 votes to one Reprefentative. In the next view, the Difproportion and Inequality of it's Diftribution encreafes: For nearly a *fourth* part of the whole Votes or 43,000, are employed in electing nearly a *tenth* part of the Houfe of Commons, or 52 Members for Cities and the Univerfities. Here the Proportion is of about 827 Votes to one Reprefentative. Go a ftep further, and the refult will be more extraordinary: For a number not fo large as the one laft mentioned, or 41,000 Electors, abfolutely return 369 Members for Towns and Boroughs, which is very nearly *two thirds* of the whole Houfe of Commons. Here the Proportion of Suffrages is about 111 to one Reprefentative. But the Inequality is not yet feen compleatly: For out of that Houfe you may felect *fifty* Members, or a *feventh* part of the whole, who are returned by 340 Electors, which conftitute only a 587th part of the whole Body in the Kingdom. Here the Proportion is of *one* Reprefentative to about *fix* votes. Take one view more: You may felect 257 Members, which make a majority of the whole Englifh Houfe of Commons, and the efficient Reprefentation of above *five millions* of People, returned by only *fix thoufand* Suffrages, which form a

E   majority

majority of the Voters in one hundred and twenty-nine of the Boroughs. So that a majority of Members may be found in the Houſe of Commons, returned by leſs than *twenty-four* Votes, on an average, to every Member.

Elected.   On the ſide of the *Elected*, the Inequality is equally glaring. If only *one* out of *ſix* enjoys the common Birth-right of Suffrage, we ſhall find only *one* out of *four* in the whole Houſe of Commons returned, in the way that a National Repreſentation ſhould be, from conſiderable communities or general portions of the People. For theſe we properly look to Counties; from whence we obtain but 92 out of 558—merely a *ſixth* part : And if to theſe we add what are returned from all the Cities and the Univerſities, amounting to 52 more, we ſhall then have but a *fourth* part of the whole. The reſt is made up from local and particular intereſts, which, by means of various interfering conſiderations, cannot be conſidered as blended with the general Voice of the People.

This very trifling Portion too in the *Elected*, which the larger communities poſſeſs, is equally irregular in it's diſtribution with the Right of Suffrage above-mentioned. Neither according to Property, nor according to Population, is it apportioned. No proof is neceſſary, that many Counties, whoſe Extent, Property, Population, and conſequently Contributions to the Taxes bear no proportion to thoſe of others, return notwithſtanding a number of Repreſentatives equal with the latter, and ſometimes infinitely greater, including the Members for the Boroughs. *Cornwall*, for inſtance, which ranks in the comparative view of it's importance as 1 to 9,

ſends

fends above *five* times as many Members to Parliament as *Middlefex*, which, including it's two cities contains a tenth part of the People, and pays the *half* of fome fubfidies, a *third* of others, and lefs than a *feventh* of none.

Is this fit to be called a National Reprefentation?

A fenfible and unprejudiced mind, which takes in the intereft of a whole, will be chagrined to think that what gives the foundation, and forms the fecurity, of the People's fhare in their own Government, is become thus ruinoufly difordered, fo as not to preferve even the form that fhould give it it's name. The Man, who reveres the Britifh Conftitution, after viewing the depredations it has fuftained in this quarter, will wonder to hear that it is ftill made the fubject of undiminifhed admiration and boaft from modern, as well as ancient, panegyrifts. They pay honors to the dead, not to the living. This branch of it however is moft certainly defunct. Or, if any virtue remains, the foreign *fcions* that have been engrafted on it, have abforbed it all— * *fcions* of wildeft ftock, married to this gentle limb, have made a bark of nobleft race conceive by buds of bafeft kind. Moft undoubtedly the *democratic* virtue of this branch has been nearly drained by the abforbing powers of the *regal* and *ariftocratic :* That diftinctive fpirit, which characterifed the popular influence, is gone : That great line, which marked the third eftate in the Government, is no longer vifible : That admirable poife, which kept the other component parts in perfect ballance, now kicks the beam. Men may admire it : But they admire it upon

* Shakefpeare's *Winter's Tale*, reverfed.

paper,

paper; they admire it at too great a diftance. Let them take a nearer view of it, let them look into it's interior compofition, and fee what paffes within it, and their admiration will unqueftionably abate much both of it's ardour and it's juftice. Even the boaft, which is in truth yet happily referved to us in the wife, and mild, and equal adminiftration of juftice, through all it's invaluable parts, muft be dependent, for the permanency of it's triumph, on the pure prefervation of thefe Legiflative Rights; amidft the growing corruption of which we have not been without the danger of feeing the line of conftitutional law, in very tender inftances, perverted, where the perverfion would give prerogative, or the fervants of it, an advantage over the country.

When therefore we hear it urged as an argument againft going into a Reform of the REPRESENTATION, that "the Conftitution has ftood hitherto as it is, and "therefore may well be left as it is, without feeking to "mend or alter it;" this is entirely begging the queftion, and begging it at fo great an expenfe to the underftanding, but however to the political knowledge, of him who ufes the argument, that I fhould be inclined to fear he chofe to *devote* the reputation of his *knowledge*, for the fuccouring of his *prejudices*. Whether the REPRESENTATION, as it now ftands, has the *Conftitution* on it's fide, can give no man, that wifhes to know it, much trouble to be informed. If it has, then what a celebrated writer * has obferved, that the rough draft of this Conftitution *was formed in the woods*, fhall be granted in the utmoft force of the idea: For certainly nothing can be

* Montefquieu.

more

more rude, undigested, wild, and horrid, than the prefent formation of the Houfe of Commons: And then it becomes a civilized and enlightened age, experiencing it's grofs defects and diforders, to give it improvement. If it has not, the fame conclufion muft follow *a fortiori:* There cannot be a fhadow of argument, why diforders, which have nothing to plead but their own vicioufnefs, fhould be continued to difhonor the wifdom, and endanger the welfare, of the fociety. In the mean time the prefumption will remain in my favor, that the truth lies in the negative; for which I fhall reft myfelf on one of the ableft authorities* in this or any age, whofe words are univerfal nature itfelf; " In the beft conftituted ftate " there is a perpetual accumulation of fomething, which " will require reform; for which reafon there is a ne- " ceffity of often recurring to firft principles."

But fome perhaps are content to look no further than the *law* and the *habits* of the times, and to take thefe, as they find them, for the Conftitution. They know that ever fince the 8 *Hen.* 6. the right of fuffrage in counties has been confined to Freeholders poffeffing at leaft 40s. *per ann.* and that from time more immemorial than that the Houfe of Commons has been filled, by a great majority, with members for particular Boroughs. They will therefore take it for granted, that the inequality we have before defcribed, both as to the *Electors* and the *Elected*, grows from the Conftitution itfelf. It will not be amifs that we beftow fome confiderations here on each of thofe points, from whence this idea arifes.

Neither Law nor Habits neceffarily make the Conftitution.

* Lord Camden.

The

The 8 *Hen.* 6. while it threw the franchife of voting into the hands of a particular clafs of men, was indeed a law of general *disfranchifement*; the firft that ever was attempted; and a bold and daring one it was. Till that moment the right of fuffrage was as univerfal as the outlines which we have before given to it: It adhered to the inhabitants of this country as *free men*; it knew nothing of them as *Freeholders*. But before we fpeak more decifively upon it, let us know the reafon or pretence for it's innovation, which it will be moft indulgent to the act to take from it's own preamble.

Two caufes are affigned therein. Firft, " that elec- " tions of Knights had been made by exceffive numbers, " many of them of fmall fubftance, yet pretending to a " right equal to the beft Knights and Efquires," Is it poffible that the fupreme Council of a free country could make fuch unfit and imprudent language it's own. Yes, God forbid! that the man of fmall fubftance fhould not pretend to as much right as his proudeft fuperior, for the protection of what is as dear to him, and in his clafs as ufeful to the country, as the other's more boafted greatnefs. Here feems to be the fad beginning of that Ariftrocatic fpirit, which hath ever been unfriendly, nay contemptuous, to the people at large. But let us proceed.

The preamble next alledges, that in confequence of thefe exceffive numbers, " Riots, Batteries, and Divifions " were very likely to arife, unlefs due remedy were " provided."

It is fomething, that the act could only fay, thefe confequences were *likely* to arife. So then, from the
poffibility

possibility that these excesses might happen, or, had they even happened, from causes no worse than *numbers*, the Freemen of England were to be bereaved of their Birth-right. Of all the pretences, which Aristocratic guile ever framed for narrowing the principles of the common People, none were ever so flimsy and so barefaced as this; which leaves us in surprize, how a law built on such pretences could ever have been attempted upon a People, or suffered by that People to gain a footing, but that they wanted education and a knowledge of their rights. Were it indeed a matter of as important *etiquette* to preserve decorum in a Country-Hustings, as in the Drawing-room of a Palace, *Henry* might be indulged in regulating the one, with no more notice than has been taken of the more courtly *Charles*, for limiting the number that should croud the royal apartments on presenting popular petitions. But the business is infinitely too serious. Nor does the cause, however menacing, justify the measure adopted, or render it necessary. They needed but to have hit upon a small part of what a very enlightened and firm friend[*] to the Constitution has lately proposed to Parliament, and all the evil they dreaded would at once have been avoided. Let them have divided the Counties into Districts, and taken the poll by ballot, and there would have been an end of *Riots*, *Batteries*, and perhaps of *Divisions*.

But if the measure taken by that act was as needless as it was wrong, what has it done to the country? No stride upon the constitution can well be spoken of more enormous. It changed the whole condition and capacity of our first and most natural franchise. It effected at once that

[*] Lord Mahon.

that inequality in the *Reprefentation* of which we complain; it robbed five parts in fix of the people of England of that inherent birth-right, by the lofs of which they became as much aliens to the kingdom and it's government, except in bearing all the burdens of it, as if they had never fet their feet upon it's foil. On thefe accounts it was unconftitutional in the extreme, and ought not to have been endured a moment; nor fhould it now, any more than if it had been an exprefs annihilation of all the privileges fecured by *Magna Charta.*

Yet let us be rightly poffeffed of the principle: It was an infufferable violation of the conftitution, but not merely as *an Act of Disfranchifement.* Such an act may be moft purely conftitutional, where it fprings from a care of that great principle, which, as I have fhewn before, reafon eftablifhes as the boundary of this and every other civil privilege; and that is, where the condition of the individual, leaving him not properly *free* to think and act for himfelf, would tend to fubvert the public good propofed by the privilege. In this cafe, to *disfranchife* is to *maintain freedom* on it's own bafis. Of this kind is an act of the laft feffion of Parliament, difabling revenue-officers, while they continue in their offices, from voting at elections; which, if it be called an Act of *Disfranchifement,* though it is but in fact a *Sufpenfion* of their franchife, is moft perfectly agreeable to the conftitution, and feeks to preferve the fpirit of it in the pureft manner: For here the right of fuffrage was become overladen with an influence, which, though not precifely marked by any characters of original difability expreffed in the conftitution, was more fore and intenfe on the individual, and left him lefs free, than any other influence that had been defcribed;—it involved all that

could

could arife from indigence, fervitude, and nonage put to-gether, to annihilate the freedom of the mind; and, there-fore, though the *Reprefentation* fhould receive the moft ample enlargement, this fhould ever continue a difability, added to thofe which reafon and the Conftitution had before expreffed; for it muft ever be unreafonable and unfafe to truft the freedom of others to him who has no freedom of his own. **The** 8 *Hen.* 6. **was** then un-**juftifiable,** becaufe it was not founded on the prefervation of this great principle; it was by no means of this pure **complexion**; it had no fhare in this conftitutional teft **and vindication of disfranchifement.** There was no pretence for faying, that they whom it difabled were not *free*; it was the avowed language of it's own preamble, that they were *too free.* This act, therefore, gave a wound to the Rights of Englifhmen, which nothing can heal but it's own annihilation—a wound which has become deeper and forer by the variety of laws relating to Elec-tions, which have all built on this defective foundation, and by that means have added accumulation to the mif-chief. That time hath given it a fanction, will make no difference to an honeft mind, which will reflect, that it is impoffible to recover a pure fyftem by compromifing with thofe vicious introductions of principles, that fuf-fered it no longer to be what it was.

But perhaps the cafe of Boroughs may appear more innocent. If thefe greatly preponderate over the more general Reprefentation—if they admit to a right of fuffrage thofe who by the laft mentioned act are excluded from it in counties—if they convert what fhould be a popular Re-prefentation into that of a few, perhaps of a family, per-haps of an individual—yet they ftand on a ground, which probably **may prefent them to us in a more** legitimate view.

Boroughs have more defe fible, but f

F

I am

I am not infenfible that they are defended by circumftances of too peculiar a caft for a formal argument to
impugn. It is not my intention to throw them into diforder. I fhall be content that the beft ufe be made of
their prefent poffeffion of the Commons-Houfe, where
that cannot be better difpofed of, without ruffling that
Houfe and the national Reprefentation too much. I am
led to fpeak of them here only in fuch meafure as may
tend to fix right ideas of the Conftitution, or to prevent
wrong ones : and to this meafure of obfervation the moft
interefted man fhould not have any objection.

Boroughs have very great antiquity on their fide. I
know there are Boroughs by prefcription, whofe commencement can be referred neither to time nor inftrument. But when we have faid this, I verily believe we
have faid all ; yet it is no trifle to be poffeffed of this
circumftance. There is a *facra ærugo*, with which antiquity encrufts things, and which, while it is convenient
to cover blemifhes, men of the beft fenfe will hefitate
moft to rub off, from a refpectful reverence, not always
abfurd, for antiquity itfelf. But the cafe before us hath
been affifted with more than the dead ruft of antiquity.
Venerable lawyers have tranfmitted through the fucceffions of time, and generally with refpectful mention,
that exercife of the royal pleafure which gave Boroughs
their birth. Let us not wonder that our kings, after the
Conqueft, affumed that exercife, when they derived it,
with the other maxims of Government, and their own
origin too, from *France*. Let us not wonder that lawyers,
taking their principles of Conftitution, as well as of common legal exercife, from precedents, fhould pafs them
down without impeachment. There is no clafs of men,

(with

(with but very few exceptions, which have chiefly been the bleffings of the laft hundred years, and the moft valuable of them the bleffings of our own day) who have in all periods done more mifchief to the country, than thefe profeffors of the *black letter*; which not unfitly characterizes the dark ill-favoured times, and the unequal affumptions of power, whofe regifters it kept to embarafs conftitutional adjuftments for endlefs generations. Let us not wonder that the People made no difficulties or objections here: *Boroughs* * were the original device of *Lewis the Grofs*, to lift the meaner People into protection from their lords, by certain privileges and a feparate jurifdiction: In *England* it raifed at firft into confideration and honor thofe who, living in a low neighbourhood together, without any particular civil tie, were in a ftation little better than fervile: And afterwards, when the *Reprefentation* came to be more regularly formed, the precedents, by which their own rank had profited fo much, became too ftrong for any exceptions that improved good fenfe, courage, or policy, peradventure emerging, could make to their continuance.

We will not therefore difturb the general acquiefcence, by difputing in the leaft the regal title to make *Corporations*; which, fays one of thefe refpectable lawyers†, *the King may do every day*; and, fays another‡, *he may make as many of them as he will*§. But if *the king may do it every day*, *in what numbers* he will, and with all the prefent confequences of making *Boroughs* (which

* Du Cange's Gloff. in verb. *Communitas.*
† Finch's Law, cap. *Franchifes.*
‡ Bacon's Difc. on Government 2d part, page 76.
§ As the Pope did Bifhops in the Council of *Trent.*

is their meaning) it is high time for us in this inquisitive age to pause, and look at the authority. And a very short distinction will separate the chaff from the wheat. Doubtless the king may create what *Corporations* he will; but to invest them with a power of sending Members into the Commons-House, without the assent of the Commons, is not his to give *de jure*, how often foever it may have been done *de facto*. If his it be to give, then is that affembly dependent indeed upon him, by what conftitutes of all things the fulleft and jufteft dependence, *Creation* itfelf: and his *Right* being maintained by fo unimpeachable a character to be *divine* over the whole affembly of the People, there can be but little colour or encouragement for individuals to refift the claim in any other quarter.

But how can the mind bring itfelf to the idea, that He on whofe power the Affembly of the Commons was meant to be a check, fhould be enabled to give that Affembly it's members in what numbers, and gathered from what fituations, he pleafes? If it has the Rights of a feparate Eftate, thofe Rights can never grow from any other than itfelf. Shall a ftranger direct me to the quarter from whence thofe are to be taken, who fhall become the truftees of my own interefts? It muft be prepofterous to conceive, that the popular authority, which gave the Crown it's prerogatives, fhould be neceffitated to depend for it's maintenance on the gratuitous re-extenfion of what it had beftowed; that the currents, which rofe from itfelf, muft return back to feed the fource which enabled them to flow. If the Crown might increafe the Reprefentatives of boroughs, no good reafon, which goes farther than a difference, with fome novelty, in the means, feems eafily to be affigned, why it might not add of itfelf to the

Members

Members for Counties. And then where may the line be drawn to the extent of that Affembly; when not only every extenfion that is given to it is derived from favor, which carries the probability of a feparate interest; but thofe, for whofe account it is profeffedly given, have not the power of judging either of the whole extent, or on the due proportions which may appear to them proper to be affigned to the various combinations of interefts, which form that auguft and extenfive truft?

Thefe circumftances have all been felt, and from the fingle caufe at prefent before us, The royal favor, extended frequently to focieties of it's own tenants and dependents, has given the Houfe of Commons at leaft three parts out of four of it's Members: hence the numbers poured in by the Charters of Incorporation from *Cornwall*, the Demefne of the Crown, which having fent twelve members, in the time of *Edward* I. has now increafed her amount to forty-four. Amidft thefe things the People experienced nothing but fluctuation in their own affembly. *Hen.* VI. privileged 17 Boroughs: *Edw.* VI. 22: *Hen.* VIII. 17: *Mary*, 14: *Eliz.* 31: and *James* I. 14. Perhaps it is not the leaft misfortune attending thefe events, that the People, as unfufpicious of confequences as they were inattentive to the power affumed, fuffered the foundation of that inequality in their own Reprefentation thus to rife, which has been the bane of their interefts through every fucceeding generation.

But to the dead all remarks are vain: We look forward to the living for their ufe. If the Conftitution be thus unfavorable to Borough Reprefentations, it

A glorious Patriotifm in thofe that can give them up.

refts

rests with the patriotism of those individuals, on whom those local interests have devolved, and of the Commons at large, by ceding those personal aggrandisements to the love of their country, to relieve the freedom of it's Parliamentary Exertions from a weight that has ever born it down, and to amputate the branches that have hung so long decayed and rotten by it's side. Where by burgage-tenures these are become a property in individuals, unquestionably the cession of them should be induced by the most ample compensation; which the keepers of the public purse would find the most advantageous and most thankful mode of employing a part of the national resources; and being offered, would certainly leave those who should refuse it, to an issue the most unpleasant of any that could possibly attend virtuous men, and honorable citizens. For the rest which are more open, and therefore may truly be considered as public Property, (I speak not here of the larger Towns or Cities) less delicacy is needful. And the Public may derive a better use from the same numbers thrown into the counties at large. It would be a glorious æra for Britain, amidst all her distresses, could she see that day. Nor would they share least in the glory, who, by the disinterested surrender of private distinctions, or rather the exchange of them for more public enjoyments, should shew themselves capable of preferring to all selfish considerations a participation with their fellow citizens in the perennial lustre of national Freedom. They would become immortal in record. They would be entitled to a civic crown; for they saved the Constitution of their Country, and with it their Country itself, at their own expence. And if a further argument be necessary to a patriot mind, neither they nor their posterity need to fear, that having waved these personal advantages, they

shall

fhall be undiftinguifhed in the larger circles of intereft. For the Man of Public Spirit, the Man of Confideration in his Neighborhood, the Man of great Abilities, the Honeft Man, the Man of Senfe, will more furely be looked for, and more highly eftimated, by the Public, when his influence and abilities can be put to no other account than the difinterefted fervice of his Country. And the applaufe he will then obtain, will not be the folitary echo of his own pride, exulting in it's exclufive power, nor the flattery of thofe who enjoy it at fecond hand, or of thofe few who are the humble inftruments of giving it effect ; but it will be the applaufe of extenfive communities, whofe partiality is judgment, and whofe weight makes honor fterling.

CHAP. III.

The PERNICIOUS CONSEQUENCES *of an unequal Re-*
prefentation, in the nature of things.

Reprefentatives of fmall local interefts never think of being
accountable—fuch are conflant materials for Minifters
to work with—a fingular apo'ogy for Boroughs an-
fwered—the danger of an unequal Reprefentation illu-
ftrated in a ftriking inftance—others more to be dreaded
equally poffible.

An unequal
Reprefentation
mifchievous in
the nature of
things.

IF the Reprefentation, which appears thus grofsly defective and abhorrent from the fpirit of the Conftitution, affected us only as we fhould be grieved to fee a
noble piece of architecture, or other compleat work of
art, defaced and mangled in ruins; we might bear with
what gave diftrefs only to our tafte. But our feelings
are of an infinitely feverer kind. In ftating the pernicious
confequences arifing from the Reprefentation as it ftands,
it may be thought that we have faid enough even in the
fhort detail we have given of the conduct of the Houfe
of Commons for the laft fourteen years. To thofe, who
are capable of conviction, it cannot be neceffary to
accumulate further proofs. But it may be conceived
that thofe meafures were the accidental events of the
time, and fprung from the peculiar fuccefsfulnefs of a
peculiar Minifter in managing the Houfe of Commons.
We fhall therefore add fome obfervations to fhew that,
in the nature of things, the prefent Reprefentation muft
be a continual invitation to the feductions of bad Minifters,

flers, and a continual temptation to the Reprefentative
Body to liften to thofe feductions.

If we are to retain the idea of any account to be
rendered by our Reprefentatives, certainly that account
will be moft likely to be kept in mind, when they feel
themfelves dependant for their truft on larger and more
general communities, undiminifhed by thofe diftinctions
of property, which tend to lofe the right idea of a
Community. For no perfonal favor can be depended
on to carry away Communities like thefe from their natural judgment of things. But when we look for the
Reprefentatives of *England*, we muft not go to larger
Communities, but to nooks and corners, for at leaft
three-fourths of their number. And what can thefe
nefts of intereft produce, but Corruption, or an unawed
Capacity of it, thro' every ftage of the bufinefs, and in all the
perfons concerned? What reftraints can he have, from the
fenfe of a Conftituent Body over him, who is returned only
by a handful of Electors? The queftion advances ftill progreffively in it's force, fhould thofe Electors be his own
friends or dependents; fhould their title to fuffrage be his
own eftate; fhould they be his own family; fhould they
be only an individual or two, created for the moment
by himfelf; fhould there not be a fingle one to be reprefented, but merely a defpicable fpot of earth, or a
few antiquated ftones in the wall. Let meafures as fervile to thofe of whom he fhould have been jealous, and
as ruinous to the nation at large, as can be conceived,
have marked the progrefs of his parliamentary truft, not
a thought of thofe, to whofe voice he goes back for a
renewal of that truft, occupies his mind. Why fhould
it? The account he has to give amounts to nothing; it
never can amount to more, where, fuppofing fome in

Reprefentatives of fmall local interefts never think of being accountable.

G   thefe

thefe confined circles intelligent and difpofed to afk
queftions, private influence can eafily ftop thefe little
currents, or divert them into it's own prevailing channel.

Here then is a direct nurfery of mifchief to the Country. Here is a ftanding fupply of materials for every
minifter, with which he may execute his plans, and on
which he makes a very ferious reckoning, when he enters
on this arduous field. I muft not blame him, as things
ftand; he cannot do otherwife, with affurance to the
public bufinefs: However, to hold himfelf fuperior to
all compacted dependance on their fupport, he muft be
caft in a mould of talents, integrity, and good fortune,
of which this country hath yet feen but one minifterial
original in the immortal *William Pitt*. With thefe inftruments he may go on even againft the fenfe of the nation
given by thofe Reprefentatives that moft properly exprefs it. This is a calamitous effect of thefe partial and
local interefts, which every Minifter that ufes them acknowledges at the time in every ftronger meafure of Government. No man looks on their fupport in the fame fatisfactory view as on that which is given by the Members
for Cities and Counties; and therefore no Minifter, contemplating any daring meafures, ever brought them forward, till he could give himfelf the confidence of finding
at leaft fome fhare of the latter in the fupport of his
views. Of this let the prefent American war give the
proof. For fometime an embrio of the Cabinet, it burft
not it's fhell, till fome part of the *Country Gentlemen*,
properly fo called, or County Members, were brought to
favor it's birth, and fofter it's growth. With the fanction
of thefe, the fact will juftify me in afferting, that this
deplorable war, deprecated, execrated, difavowed by the
far greateft part of the nation, rufhed into being infinitely
stronger

ftronger and better-favored in the Minifter's eyes, than
if it had been legitimated by the concurrent voice of
King, Lords, and Commons, the *Country Gentlemen* being
no part of the approving number.

We repeat it therefore again, here is a direct nurfery
of mifchief to the country. An apology has lately been
attempted for thefe local infractions into an equal Reprefentation, by an ingenious Gentleman *, who has given
a different turn to their effects. He fays, " they are an
" ufeful nurfery for bringing forward fucceffions of ge-
" nius to Parliamentary dignity." This is undoubtedly
original. No foil lefs fertile than his own could have conceived it. Whether he means to tell us, that Genius is
a Plant, which thrives beft under partial funs, with more
limited culture, and in a foil confined, where fewer
means contribute to pufh it's rifing head into all it's full-
blown honors, I leave to his own explanation; in the
forming of which a moment's retrofpect on the experienced climes of *Malton* and of *Briftol* will not be amifs.
Or, would he infinuate that the fituations, which are
favorable to *Country-Gentlemen*, will give no opening to
Genius? Or, are we to underftand, that adventuring
abilities are falutary to the politics and the good of a
country, and ought to be encouraged at every confequence? In my opinion, though the encouragement of
Genius be the moft honorable idea in the human mind,
yet in a political line the good of it is equivocal to the
conftitution and the country. The former cannot commonly need it: That is fixed and certain, and prefers it's
own plain and ftable principles to all brilliancy of colou-

A fingular apo-
logy for Bo-
roughs anfwer-
ed.

* Mr. B—e, in a late fpeech in the Houfe of Commons.

G 2

ing. The latter muſt wiſh for ever to be the nurſe of talents, from whence ſhe may derive not leſs intrinſic advantage than ſplendor in all her contingences : But ſhe may alſo be ruined by the ambition of thoſe talents, or the wrong prejudices they take, both in the important intereſts that are agitated for the time, and in her conſtitution for ever. In the caſe of that Honorable Gentleman himſelf to whom I allude, if thoſe talents, whoſe introduction into Parliament he has modeſtly quoted as a proof of the utility of Boroughs, had been as friendly to the People's ſhare in the Conſtitution, as they are enviable in general learning, perhaps the objections to his apology had not now preſented themſelves ſo ſtrong : certainly it would have been a pleaſure to have ſeen that a mind, ſo elegant in other reſpects, was not marred by a fatal want of judgment, and by a palpable ſacrifice of it's ſenſe to it's paſſions, in every thing that concerns the Rights of his fellow Citizens.

The apology therefore of that Gentleman is ſomewhat too viſionary, if not too vain ; and I muſt beg the Reader's pardon for having been a little viſionary in following him. I will ſuggeſt to him a more natural and real tendency, to which theſe local Repreſentations ſerve : and my idea ſhall have nothing viſionary, but what we ſee and feel, and have been ſickening under for an age. They are nurſeries for jobbers, placemen, penſioners, dependants, tools, and adventurers of every kind ; for all, who have got a notion of the Trade of Parliament ; or, in other words, who are content to ſerve, and wiſh to be ſerved themſelves ; for all, who ſeek to prey upon the vitals of the Country ; all, who have preyed on them, and wiſh to be ſcreened by Miniſters ; all, who cannot hope to obtain from a diſcerning people at large the
very

very important truft of deciding in all that is dear to a people.

I return therefore once more o my affertion, here is a direct nurfery of mifchief to the Country. If from the habit of feeing thefe effects, they lofe the appearance of abufes, and diminifh our apprehenfions of their danger, let a ftranger, who is under no prejudices of the place to take off from the credit of his report, come forward to fhew what is to be dreaded—a ftranger, who has feen to another end of the earth the opportunity that is given, by the prefent ftate of our Reprefentation, to the playing of any game upon Parliament by thofe whofe intereft is of magnitude enough to induce it.

The danger of an unequal Reprefentation illuftrated in a ftriking inftance.

An Afiatic Prince, the Nabob of *Arcot*, finding that the concerns of his extenfive territories were likely to change hands from the India Company to the Parliament of *England*, foon catches the fyftem by which a door may be opened for the introduction of his own importance into that Affembly. He opens his coffers: He tranfmits a fum of money fufficient to purchafe eight or nine of thefe local Reprefentations, which are filled with men infeparably connected with his interefts. Whom do thefe men reprefent? Any part of the People of England? No. The Nabob of *Arcot*. And the feats they hold have more immediate reference to the dominions of *Indoftan*, than to the empire of *Britain*. *India* is far more virtually reprefented by them than five-fixths of the People of *England* are in their own Houfe of Commons. Does not this inftance ftrike us with confufion? How horrid, how intolerable, muft be the Reprefentation of a Country that can give room, and fo eafily, fo conftantly, to a poffibility like this? Did our forefathers dream of fuch

such a thing? And will their sons, to whom so glaring a
proof of the desolation which hovers over the primary
security of all they have, is reserved—reserved in the
kindness of Providence, to give us that full sense of our
situation, from which there is no retreating—will they,
either from an indifference to what is best for them, or
from the interruptions of private interests, suffer so dis-
graceful a depravation to continue of what any country
upon earth would value beyond expression? For, supposing the Representation to rest more equally on larger
divisions of the People, is it possible for practices like
that I have mentioned to succeed? Could those men,
though Englishmen, yet unknown in *England*, or worse
than unknown, find their Elections then so easy in Counties or in many Cities? The Reform would be Death to
their hopes. It is not the revenues of a Nabob, nothing
less than the treasures of *Delhi*, could be competent to
the corruption of extended Communities, and reap any
plenteous harvest from it. And were the return of
Elections made more frequent also, even Asiatic coffers
would languish under the drains that gave them no
respite.

Others more to
be dreaded,
equally possible.

But the reasoning, which arises from this extraordinary
instance, by no means terminates with it. What an In-
dian Prince saw encouragement to attempt, may be ac-
complished more formidably by one nearer home. Suppose the Court of *France* was to take up the idea of de-
voting in this way but a very few of those millions, which
she in vain employs against us in naval exertions. As
the facility of doing it is unquestionable, so the consequences to all that is dear to us must be plain. I
believe in my conscience, that one able man in St. *Ste-
phen's* Chapel would go farther towards accomplishing her
views

views in this war than a thousand foldiers landed on this island, or a moderate ship of force added to her line. And I have not a doubt but a single million, employed with fecrecy, could make it's way on a General Election, through that vile Reprefentation of our country, fo as prefently to bring us into whatever facrifices a well-managed policy could draw from the refolves of Parliament. And can we be fatisfied to ftand in this predicament? Whether it be probable that we may ever thus fall or not, is not the queftion. The Reprefentation leaves us a prey to every invader, who may be bold enough to lay hold on us in this way: It gives an opening to any depredations, which any individual within, or any enemy without, may think worth while to attempt: At the fame time to the People at large it is the fartheft from what can deferve the name of fecurity.

CHAP. IV.

First Advantage *that will result from a reformed Represen-tation:* ARISTOCRATIC PARTY *annihilated.*

The unnatural and disproportionate grasp of Power by the Nobility—but most inordinate in those who feel the spirit of Aristocratic connections—both to the sovereign autho-rity—and also to the People—the views of Aristocracy favored by an unequal Representation; by Boroughs—more compleatly assisted by the Statute 8 Hen. VI. *by which Counties became but larger Boroughs—property the foundation and genius of Aristocracy—Similitude be-tween the Aristocratic regulation of Election by* Servius Tullus *and the statute* 8 Henry VI.—*Aristocracy by these means knit into a Faction—and uniform in the means of preserving it's power—as professing patriotic principles, these bounded by an opposition to royal prerogative—the Patriotism expected by the People broader and more radi-cal than this—the People constantly deserted by the Aristo-cratic Party on constitutional points—a tribute of respect to the private virtues of many who compose that Party—how a reform of the Representation will naturally annihi-late it—such a Faction annihilated, every branch of cha-racter will feel a new Being—the Man of Abilities—the Minister—the Crown—the Country at large—answer to part of a late Speech at Westminster—and to similar mat-ter in a Pamphlet, entitled,* Thoughts on Discontents.

IT is painful but to touch superficially the disorders arising from a subject, on which every country that would wish to be free or wise must feel with so much sensibility as on that of a national Representation: and therefore

therefore we dwelt as little as the matter would permit us on the laft part of our enquiry. We enter now on a more pleafant divifion of our fubject, the *Advantages* that will refult from a conftitutional correction of thofe diforders.

The firft advantage I fhall mention is, that it will cut up the undue influence of Ariftocratic Party by the roots.

In a difordered Government we naturally expect to find the component parts refpectively gaining or lofing fome ground upon one another. But in no Government, founded in general freedom, was there ever feen a more absolute abforption of all the genuin vigor of the other parts, by that which in effential operation was the leaft important of all, than in the ftrides and the pretenfions of that Ariftocratic Party, which has long either dictated the rule to this Country, or rendered it difficult for the executive Power to conduct it: In *Rome*, where the main Body of the Government was one, the Senate, and that Senate was all Patrician, we cannot wonder to fee the Patrician Spirit, the Patrician Power, in all things, and all things drawn into it's vortex. At *Venice*, notwithftanding her State Inquifitors, and her diftribution of the three great Powers of Government, the legiflative, the executive, and the judiciary, into three feveral tribunals; yet thefe are but fo many branches of one and the fame body, the Ariftocratic, whofe prefervation is the object of her Inquifitors, and whofe power is the center of all her tribunals; we ceafe, therefore, to be furprized that this over-ruling influence leaves the Doge a fhadow, and the People a cypher. But in *England* the Conftitution has taught us to look on the Nobility with a different

The unnatural and difproportionate grafp o Power by th Nobility.

H   view.

view, as an important and dignified branch of the Government, but neither as original in it's confideration, nor
as extenfive in it's claims, as either of the others. 'Tis
therefore more enormous and unnatural, if Ariftocracy
here fhould become predominant; if like that of *Venice*,
it fhould make the Monarch a Doge; or, like that of
Genoa, it fhould leave to the people only the importance
of adminiftring the Bank of St. *George:*—an importance,
which is all, I fear, that the People of *England* can
claim, and with much difadvantage compared with that
of *Genoa:* For the latter, by adminiftring the Bank, ac-
quire a very powerful influence in the Government; the
former keep, 'tis true, the purfe of the nation, and ad-
minifter it's fupplies, but in this they are become too
much the inftruments of the Nobles, who tenacioufly
keep the key which excludes them from the emancipa-
tion that would make even this privilege of value.

It is fufficient to fay this of the Nobility as a Body.
Were we juftified in bringing the whole of it into that
combination of Ariftocracy which we have in view, and
which is very well underftood in *England*, it might be
proper to fhew the true limits of their power, by their
original deftination in the monarchy, and the portion of
check which is given them in the legiflative counfels.
This is not neceffary here. Yet we cannot equally pafs
over other circumftances which, whether they naturally
apply to all that are ennobled, I will not fay, but certainly
they form a very ftriking feature in thofe, whether within
the Body of Nobility or out of it, whofe minds feel the
fpirit of Ariftocratic connexion, and are formed to the
habits of it. What I mean is this: There is no de-
fcription of men in a ftate, who are lefs inclinable than
thefe to keep within due limits, more difpofed to enlarge
their

their ſtrides, and more tenacious to maintain thoſe ſtrides
they have taken. A glare of greatneſs, which pure de-
mocracy expeĉts not, and therefore does not feel, and
which royalty thinks not of, becauſe a much purer ſplendor is inſeparable from it, impels the mind wedded to
Ariſtocratic connexions to make the compaſs of it's power
as large as the paſſion which fills it. Hence it often happens by an unhappy fatality to the royal fountains of honor, that the ſtreams they give turn back to pollute their
head: Kings, as well as a greater Creator, give an honorable exiſtence to many beings, to receive annoyance
in return. They array themſelves with ſatellites, but to
rob their planet of it's luſtre. Theſe are not mere images Both to the ſo
vereign autho-
rity.
in the hiſtory of nations. In every monarchy that hath
been known, Ariſtocratic faĉtions have left indelible
marks of their unſatiated views; not merely to give limitation to the ſovereign authority, but to render themſelves independent of it, or even to extinguiſh it. Thus
the Kings in ancient *Italy*, and ancient *Greece*, were at laſt
deſtroyed and exterminated. In more modern times, the
ſame powerful faĉtions ſucceſſively overturned the numerous monarchical ſovereignties, which had been raiſed in
Italy on the ruins of the Roman empire, or eſtabliſhed in
other parts of *Europe*. Look, for inſtance, to *Sweden*,
Denmark, and *Poland*: There faĉtions of Nobles have
commonly reduced their Sovereigns to the condition of
ſimple preſidents over their aſſemblies, and mere often-
ſible heads of the government. If in *Germany* and *France*
the monarchs proved better able to maintain themſelves
againſt the ſame combinations, it can only be aſcribed to
the ſtrength they received from their conſiderable demeſnes. Thus it has fared with monarchs in all ages,
from Ariſtocratic faĉtions. Whether the People have And alſo to the
People.
had leſs to complain of, let the hiſtory of every country

H 2   under

under Heaven, whether Monarchic or Republican, bear witnefs. I afk not that you fhould fingle out the opprefſions, the feceſſions of the People, the general convulſions, which the Ariſtocratic ſpirit hath produced. This were to take the moſt unfavorable view of it, as enforced by *bad* men in it's extremes. But look at it's complexion in better times, and in the hands of better characters. Recollect the embarraſments with which, in moments the moſt trying to a public ſpirit, they have clogged not only the national intereſts, but the fovereign authority, on any acuter jealouſics of power: and in this account let not the memorable events which our own country will furniſh in the years 1746, and 1782, be forgotten. The faſt is: If they have not oppreſſed, yet they never would relieve, where the relief would leſſen their own ſway. They might poſſibly loofen fome fhackles impofed by another power, but they were never known to relax their own. In this cafe they changed hands, but no more. If they releafed the People from a *Pharaoh* and his tafk-maſters, they became the tafk-maſters and the *Pharaoh* themfelves. The reafon is, Diſtinction is their principle. They cannot level themfelves to equal participation. Let a moſt refpectable authority * clofe thefe remarks with a characteriſtic of the Ariſtocratic temper, which comes home to all we have faid. *This ſpirit* (fays he) *may think it an honour to obey a king, but conſiders it as the loweſt difgrace to fhare the power with the People.*

If this is the natural turn of the Ariſtocratic ſpirit, circumſtances of long tenure in the legiſlative power of this country have lent it abundant gratification. In ad-

* Monteſq. Spirit of Laws, vol. 1. p. 151.

verting

verting to thefe circumftances, our attention will be brought back to the great national evil, which is the object of our writing.

In the unequal Reprefentation of the People we fhall find the caufe which hath lifted up the Ariftocracy of *England*, and lifted it into faction. What do we call a Faction, but the power of a part, ufurping what is of more diffufive Right, and counteracting the more general intereft for the fecurity of itfelf? Let us watch the progrefs of Ariftocracy in *England*, by this rule.

The views of Ariftocracy favored by an unequal Reprefentation.

The moment a Borough was created, and not in a great city, a foundation was laid for fubjugating a whole People to the power of a few. For a feries of time the evil lurked unfeen. Even when the extenfion was made to greater numbers, the power conveyed refted with the incorporated individuals, or thofe that filled their places. But prefently this muft abide other events in the revolution of things. The great man rifes. The rich man becomes confpicuous. Ambition points out to each the flattering confequence that awaits political diftinction. Their grafp is opened to the means; and in the change, which time has introduced into private Incorporations, they find them. Is the power annexed to tenure? It becomes the object of purchafe, and wealth makes it it's own. Is it annexed to partial Election? Surrounding property, and furrounding influence, ftill fpread a net from which it is not eafy to efcape; till as time and fome variation of circumftances ftrengthen opportunities, that which refted in a few unconnected perfons is transferred to the dependents, or perhaps to the family, of a potent individual.

By Boroughs.

Thus

Thus by degrees Boroughs came to acknowledge private lords, instead of public objects; and by this mean a very large share of political importance was acquired at once, not only by those who meant to figure high by this interest in the Assembly of the Commons, but by many Peers, who had caught the idea, that without this branch of Parliamentary interest, even their nobility left their weight in the State too sensibly defective. But this is no tall. The importance, which was then opened to the Great, became encreased and confirmed by that infamous statute passed in the 8 *Hen.* VI. which without reason, or pretence of reason, threw the Right of suffrage in Counties from *men* to *property.* This act was as it were a call upon Aristocracy to rear up it's head : And from this moment it felt itself erect ; it became fortified. Some outworks it had obtained before, but now a line of circumvallation was compleated around it. By that line the most extensive scale of Parliamentary Representation was brought into a more convenient compass for the personal influence of powerful individuals to turn to their own advantage. Even Counties were now rendered but a larger sort of Boroughs. By narrowing the power of Election within lesser numbers, and so much lesser as it was then reduced to, that power was evidently brought within the nearer reach of property : and by confining it to property alone, it was in a manner thrown into the hands of those who should possess a large share of the Country, if not by what they possessed, or by portions carved out of it, yet by the influence that is inseparably attached to it.

More compleatly assisted by the Stat. 8. Hen. VI. by which Counties became but larger Boroughs.

Property the foundation and genius of Aristocracy.

The fact is, that property is the very genius of Aristocracy ; this has it's foundation therein, it cannot thrive upon any other system, but that which is partial to property. And therefore in every age, and every Country

upon

upon earth, which has been favorable to Aristocratic views, the laws, or at least the internal regulations, have ever manifested a strong bent to give property the advantage over every other Circumstance. Let us call to mind the well-known regulation of the Right of Election by *Servius Tullus* in the very early days of *Rome.* In spirit, intention, and effects it was exactly of a piece with the statute of our *Sixth Henry* above-mentioned. He divided the People into one hundred and ninety-three Centuries, giving to each Century one vote. Now tho' ostensibly he comprised all, yet was this an arrangement of property rather than persons; and with property the whole command of Elections rested. For he appropriated ninety-eight of these Centuries to the patricians and leading men, which was giving them an absolute majority of the whole by three. But this was not all. One half of the other ninety-five he filled with Citizens of a middle class, down to the level, as we may imagine, of our Freeholders of 40s. *per ann.* For the poorer sort, comprising all that subsisted on manual labor, he threw into the remaining centuries. So that the leading men, not only by the absolute majority of their own voices, but by their influence over many in the next classes of property below them, hardly left a visible interest uncovered by themselves; and the far most numerous class of the people, though treated with some little more ceremony than the People of *England* were in our *Henry*'s reign, were, in every rational sense of things, no less disfranchised than those who fell within the scope of *Henry*'s exclusion. Had *Servius Tullus* conceived the foolish idea of a virtual Representation, possibly the little ceremony he bestowed on the bulk of his people had been spared. However, a most decided support was here given to Aristocracy, and on it's own favourite idea. The distinction was drawn between

Similitude between the Aristocratic regulation of Election by *Servius Tullus* and the Stat. 8 *Hen.* VI.

between *Perfon* and *Property*, and the preference to the latter was marked as ftrongly as art could do it. We will only obferve further, that this overbearing policy continued, till after various ftruggles by the People to break down the old preference and diftinction, and to recover *Perfons* to the confequence due to their numbers, by calling them out to vote no longer in *Centuries*, but in *Curiæ*, and afterwards by *Tribes*, it ended in the unhappy eftablifhment of the *Plebifcita* *, which was precifely tantamount to the exercife of legiflative power by our Houfe of Commons exclufive of the Peers.

Let us profit by the example. Without timely prevention it will recur for ever, in one violent fhape or another, from every people in the world capable of free fentiments, and once fenfibly touched with the difparagements eftablifhed upon them: And this timely prevention honeft men, who have the power of it, will not be backward to give. What room have we for a credit of this kind to the Ariftocratic fpirit of the Country?

Ariftocracy by thefe means knit into a faction.

Poffeffed of the advantages above-mentioned for a ftrong Parliamentary intereft, they naturally make a common caufe, and become lifted into Party, as individually they were lifted into power. The power, which aggrandifes a few at the expence of the many, calls upon thofe few to find in combination what may fuftain them againft the many. There is an everlafting jealoufy attendant on the mind, which exclufively enjoys what it ought but to participate. And when we confider that there is not a feeling in the human breaft more ardent than that of power, whenever by accident or by induftry, in mode or

* Dion. Halicarn. lib. 6. p. 410. lib. 7. p. 430. lib. 11. p. 724, 725. Livy, lib. 3.

in

in extent, we are become poffeffors of more than in natural fitnefs appertains to us, or of fo much as leaves confiderable numbers diffatisfied ; the cafe then affuredly exifts, wherein faction finds it's commencement. It muft find it in felf-love ; it will find it in felf-defence. It will find it not perhaps from hoftility to the fociety, or to thofe claffes whom it hath difparaged; but from a belief, partial to itfelf, that neither focie y, nor any of it's claffes, will be the worfe for the hands into which the power is become narrowed.

In this progrefs of felf-prefervation, as facred to it's views as what moft purely deferves the name, it will move, and ever has moved, by an uniformity of plan, attentive to every means, which can ufually make and bind a party. Among thefe we are not merely to expect thofe abler managements of times and things, which mark the great political character. Parties are ftrengthened by other things than by wifdom, or an union of manly meafures. Even the paffions are made to bend this way, and unions of a different kind occupy no trifling attention, for the political as much as the tender cement they beftow : though if this mode of ftrengthening modern Ariftocracies as well as the old had not been made the fubject of a ferious cenfure by *Montefquieu* *, we fhould have fuffered the fubfifting evidences of it to have funk in their own littlenefs, and fhould have left to the Ariftocracies of old the ungracioufnefs of rendering the moft honored of the female fex the inftruments of difparaging a people, and perpetuating obnoxious factions to the world.

And uniformity the means of preferving it's Power.

* Vol 1. page 68.

I

But

As professing
patriotic prin-
ciples, these
bounded by an
opposition to
royal preroga-
tive.

But it is not by acts of *positive* support to itself, it is by
those of a *negative* support to the country, that such a
faction presents itself in the most unfavorable view.
That man gives a negative support to any cause, who
barely does it no mischief: as he is a man of negative
virtue, who just avoids the committing of any vice. In
this idea, we pay the Aristocratic party an apparent
compliment, by supposing them by no means the enemies
of their country, but rather ostensibly it's friends. It is
best to speak out in the unequivocal simplicity of truth.
They are Whigs. As such, they possess the only principles of a just and happy administration of Government,
as settled at the Revolution, and the only cement which
can bind together an administration happy and beneficial
to this country. For the same reason they are friends to
the freedom of the Subject. But how? To Freedom, as
at the Revolution it was adjusted ; that is, as opposed to
royal prerogative. What was then gained to the Constitution, and to popular Freedom, was chiefly gained in
this view. Farther than this, or in conflict with any
other circumstances which might narrow it, the freedom
of the People found no reforms to it's extensive claims.
What gave the dimensions then to constitutional freedom,
as opposed to the Crown, gives the dimensions to the
patriotism of the Aristocratic party. In opposition to
the Crown, they are the friends of the people; they
abet the popular cause; they come forward with their
countenance, and with a willing lead, on all occasions
that take this ground, Is an administration corrupt?
They look not, they desire not to look, any farther for
the cause than to the growing influence of the Crown.
Are corrections necessary to this corruption in the very
seat of legislature? They will give it in those branches
of office, or those temporary and accidental abuses, in
whose

whofe correction the Crown will feel itfelf weakened; but the root of all, which would bring up with it abufes more inveterate, they will not fuffer to be touched. Do miferies accumulate on the Country? 'Tis the ambition of the Crown has brought them on. Is effential liberty verging to it's ruin? 'Tis the Crown alone has generated and matured the danger.

But the People look with broader views, and at the fame time more direct to the cure of their own evils. The People are ftraight in their ideas, becaufe in grievances they can have no partiality or preference: degrees of abhorrence they may have, and thefe rife higheft to the grievance that is moft radical. They know that the fame fource which gave the Crown any corrupt power in Parliament, firft gave an undue one to individuals of their fellow-fubjects. They know that were they releafed from the whole loins of the Crown, the bare hand of Ariftocratic party would leave a weight hardly lighter on their necks than thofe loins themfelves. They look therefore to the bottom of the malady. They dwell not on partial excrefcences. They feek remedies, which fhall leave the Conftitution pure. But this is friendfhip to the Country. This is difinterefted patriotifm to the whole Government. Say rather, this is death to thofe whofe power arifes from abufe, and depends for it's continuance on the exclufion of a radical reform. Let the Ariftocratic party anfwer for themfelves, how often in public conjunctures they have ftarted afide like a broken bow. How often in the numerous occafions which have brought them and the People together in the courfe of late Adminiftrations, that have unhappily filled the Country with difcontents for a courfe of years, they have deferted the public ground, when once thus broadly taken,

The Patriotifm expected by the People broader and more radical than this.

The People conftantly deferted by the Ariftocratic party on conftitutional points.

or

or have marred it by some artful measure, of more shew than moment; and thus have brought discerning men, after repeated experience of these things, to the verge of guarding a credulous Public against the patriot professions of a party, more dangerous to the People, because they rank as their friends, than those obnoxious Administrations, against which the People needed no guard, because they expected no good from their hands.

The more we were to enquire into these occasions, the less we should see of the spirit of the true English Barons, standing forth on the call of public discontents. In the great Charter they stipulated in favor even of the Bondman. But we might now more fitly conceive ourselves surrounded by the Peers of *France*, who in treaties with their princes vouchsafed not a thought about any other order than their own *.

I cannot satisfy my own mind, any more than I should satisfy my Readers, or the fit notions of justice, in having made these general reflexions, without descending to some particular references out of many that may be made. I shall keep within very recent memory. We have not forgotten what share the Aristocratic party had in the Administration of 1765. Mr, *Wilkes* will remember it. I appeal to that Gentleman for the pains which were taken to narrow the great questions that arose from his

---

* I have my eye more immediately on the famous treaty made at St. *Maur*, between Lewis 11th and the Peers of France, and which was made to terminate a war that was called a War for the Public Good. Not a single provision was included, but concerning the power of a few lords; not a word was inserted in favor of the People. This treaty may be seen at large in the *pieces justificatives* annexed to the *Memoires de Philipe de Comines*.

personal cafe, and to keep from parliamentary difcuffion every thing of a conftitutional complexion, which might embarafs, if not render precarious, the Minifterial fituation. The Adminiftration of that party was but fhort. It's oppofition feems by Fate to be everlafting. In the latter therefore we fhall have the more to refer to. Were *Calcraft* alive, he fhould fpeak. But Mr. *Sawbridge* fhall receive the appeal in his ftead. Let that Gentleman fay, and for the fake of his own principles let him not forget, who fled from the fupport of the people, thirteen years ago, in a point of the firft conftitutional magnitude, and after a folemn compact to maintain it. Mr. *Horne Tooke* could well explain what refolutions were excited by that tranfaction, and what perfuafions prevailed to confign them to filence. I appeal not to one, but to the whole Committees of *Middlefex*, *Weftminfter*, *Surry*, and *Bucks*, from what quarter proceeded the ftrenuous endeavours to confine the views of the Affociations, then newly formed, to the rubbing of the old fore of enormous influence, and the new one of enormous expenditure, in the Crown. When the Delegates met in 1780, I appeal to Mr. *Baker*, among others, for the extraneous interference, which was fo anxious to derange the conftitutional comprehenfion of their refolves, and having effected by manœuvres the over-reach of the 20th *March*, left the friends of the People to make the moft of the caufe, whofe vigour and contexture their own credulity had weakened. I forbear to appeal to the private *fcrutoire*, which may yet contain the *Memorandum* agreed on at that period by fome diftinguifhed characters, for the prefervation of good faith and a right underftanding in the furtherance of certain conftitutional reforms; or to the private memory, which can beft explain how that *Memorandum* came to be no better than wafte paper. I will not appeal to Mr.

Burke

Burke for the reafons which then brought forth his laboured Bill. All who had fenfe to obferve, and eyes to fee, might and did figure to themfelves the vanity or the tricks of a man, who, to reftore a fickly and cankered tree into health, fhould amufe himfelf and it's deluded owner with barely picking off the curled leaves and their vermin from the branches. But a later period hath feen the fame Ariftocratic party once more in poffeffion of power, which, tho' very tranfitory indeed, was long enough to afford an additional reference. I appeal to his Grace of *Richmond* for the proof of the Compact, and to the Hon. *William Pitt* for that of the Defertion.

> Pars etiam mecum quædam moriatur oportet :
> Meque velim poffit diffimulante tegi.
> Si vox in fragili mihi pectore firmior ære,
> Pluraque cum linguis pluribus ora forent ;
> Non tamen idcirco complecterer omnia verbis,
> Materia vires exfuperante meas.

Ovɪᴅ's Trift. Eleg. 5.

This is a Cabinet of Curiofities, and attended with an uncommon quality, that they are more valuable in their ufe, than pleafing to the view. The hand which expofes them does it, I am fenfible, with fome temerity, and no trifling rifque. I know full well, that the pen which writes thefe lines is fharper than the keeneft axe to cut afunder the planks of friendfhip, on which I have ftood, or thought I ftood, for twenty years. But the teft of all virtue is in the facrifices it dares to make in the day of trial. The time is now come, or never will, to fet the Conftitution and the Country on their legs ; and I embrace it.

Here

Here then is the detail of the Aristocratic Party : In the progress of which I have felt a very sensible concern, that the exposure, which I have been obliged to give of political circumstances, hath seemed for the time to throw too much out of sight the satisfaction I enjoy in contemplating and expressing the abundant private virtues that distinguish many who compose it. In the view of personal integrity, it is impossible to select better examples. The name of *Rockingham* will not obtain, from the superstitious veneration which follows the dead, more heart-felt sensations of affectionate regard than his universal goodness as a man, and the perfect integrity of all his personal transactions as a Minister, commanded when living : And I will add this further tribute to his memory, that had he been left to himself, had not his partialities listened to those, who never had his judgment, or his moderation,. or his love for his country, but thought to flatter his political .bias, or to feed their own, I have strong reasons to know that in many instances he would have bent much from the rigid policy of his party, to make the country happy. To *Portland* every mouth must give every virtue under heaven. It is impossible to say more : nor will it diminish the value of what has been said, that in the distributions of political power they had, or they have favouritisms at heart. Power is a natural exception from the general principles of passion, at least, from the strict notions of moral turpitude, into which the passions may run. From habits of sentiment however, somewhat justified by the world, if not in the purity of things, very honest and well-meaning minds may see no infringement on the rectitude of personal character in the affectations of political power. Let this apology be sufficient for their virtue. Our's, as the People, must have it's own aspect too. We may admire the goodness

A tribute of respect to the private virtues of many who compose that Party.

of

of their hearts, but we cannot confent to their dominion.
Not all the virtues they poffefs can juftify the fyftem
they would hold either over the Crown or the People.
It is unnatural in this country, and therefore ought no
longer to be known. And I muft proteft for myfelf,
feeling the duty of an Englifhman to know no powers
over him but thofe which are natural in their kind,
if I am to be narrowed in my freedom, I will
much fooner receive the reftriction from the Crown,
than from my fellow-fubjects with all their virtues on
their heads. While a trace of the monarchy is to remain, it is impoffible that a different fentiment can be
juft.

Ihw a Reform
of the Repre-
fentation will
naturally anni-
hilate it.

We are prepared now to judge of the views and effects
of Ariftocratic Party, and how far it is the intereft both
of Prince and People to annihilate it's Power. If the
queftion be afked, how will the *Reprefentation*, when
conftitutionally corrected, do this ? The anfwer is plain:
That which derives all it's advantage from the inequality
of power, muft be gone, when the Power out of which
it grows is rendered equal, or in proportion to the
equality that fucceeds. If the Great are enabled to
become a diftinct party in the country from the exiftence
of Boroughs, and from counties being made in point of
fuffrage but a larger fort of Boroughs ; either amputate or
reduce the former, and give the latter the extent of
fuffrage which befits the name, with the increafe of
Members that fhall befit their rank, and the cure of the
complaint comes naturally forward by removing what
fed the difeafe, and applying what tends to defeat it's
return. In the great mafs of people, through whom
the origin of parliamentary power fhall then be diftri-
buted, where fhall any individual of whatever rank
make

make fure of an intereſt that ſhall enable a party to rear up it's head?

Annihilate faction, and there is not a branch of cha-racter in the Country, that will not feel itſelf raiſed to a new Being, and new Capacities. The MAN OF ABI-LITIES will then come forth as he ſhould do, and take the place in his circuit which is due to abilities, and which every wiſe ſyſtem will give them. Nothing will ſtill hinder the man of rank and fortune from poſſeſſing re-ſpect, and even degrees of influence. But the fool of fortune can never ſhine at large under this reform, and much leſs lead a Country. Abilities conjoined with rank will moſt probably give not a jot leſs power than any ſuch man now enjoys: But that power will be perſonal to him-ſelf; it will neither make the head of many others, as dependent upon him, nor paſs by hereditary deſcent to thoſe that are leſs gifted. Has the Country an evident intereſt in ſuch a courſe of things, or has it not? Ought any man to look for more than in this medium is before him?

Such a faction annihilated, every branch of character will feel a new Being. The Man of Abilities.

The MINISTER will feel a ſituation, which has hardly ever been the lot of his office. If incapable or corrupt, he muſt expect a ſpeedy extinction. If he be the upright man, if he be the friend of the Country, he may bid de-fiance to every thing within the walls of Parliament that would ſhake him. For there is no power derived from the People, that ſtands now between him and that People, or between their voice and him. Faction therefore loſes it's name, or however it's effects, both in ſuccour and in terror. Where a whole nation, or the bulk of it, ſup-ports, on an enlarged ſcale of Repreſentation, with more frequent Election, whence can the oppoſition come, that

The Minister.

K   can

can be formidable or lasting? Where a whole nation, or
the bulk of it, condemns, whence can arise the party
to preserve him in the office when his power is gone?
Seated in an assembly that springs from the whole People,
he sees himself surrounded by characters, that make the
office he fills either perfectly happy, unembarrassed, and
honourable, or the forest of plagues. For they are all,
in every sense of the word, those *Country Gentlemen*,
whose voice is even now considered to sustain o. exani-
mate, as they rise individually from large portions of the
People. Or, if there still be a party there, it will be his
emulation to make it such a one as distinguish 1 the days
of the immortal *William Pitt*, when party was forced to
melt into the general voice, and uncourted poured it's
involuntary support on that genuine MAN OF THE
PEOPLE.

The Crown.

What THE CROWN will gain in circumstances not to
be impeached, nor constituting the least portion of
public advantage, we shall shew in the ensuing chapter.

The Country at large.

THE COUNTRY AT LARGE will see it's way more
fairly open to such a participation in the fruits of public
patronage, which are the common stock of the Country,
as shall respectively befit it's Individuals. Under the
prevalence of an Aristocratic party, what portion of regard doth the country obtain? What do we see that be-
speaks the first desire of an enlarged mind, possessed of the
impressions of Greatness? Such a one by a natural im-
pulse looks out for merit, brings it forward into countenance, and feels no greater pleasure from his power than
in making it the nursery of talents, which will be valuable to the Country, happy for the age, and honorable
to him that raised them. This never fails to actuate, in
a high

a high degree, every great mind, even under the peculiarities of political managements—thofe only excepted, who feel the fpirit of Ariftocratic party. What makes it's way to them muft come through an Ariftocratic medium. They transfer no countenance but to thofe, who are weighed in their own fcales, or perhaps will not bear to be weighed at all, but are the mere appendages of a party, as the faggots that make up the mufter of an army. Then no matter how well or ill-directed the patronage may be. The clumfy and illiterate are pufhed into ranks, which they know not how to fuftain; and the low unprincipled parafite eats the bread that fhould feed the independent breaft. Emoluments are crouded on individuals: nor does the overt-act fatisfy: jobs are done in fecret, for a neft to the hypocrite to every principle but the exclufive rule of his party. A Minifter, difengaged from the preffures of fuch a faction, muft feel himfelf happy. And till then he never can feel himfelf great, by that liberal exercife of the national patronage, which is moft confonant to true ambition, and alone can fatisfy the feelings of a generous mind.

But before we difmifs the Ariftocratic party, we muft beg leave to fay a few words on a very extraordinary obfervation made by a very extraordinary Gentleman * in his fpeech to the Electors of *Weftminfter*, on the 17th of laft *July*. The Obfervation I refer to is this † : " That " when the Reprefentation of the People fhall be re- " formed, it will put us more than ever to the neceffity

Anfwer to part of a late Speech at *Weftminfter*.

---

* The Hon. C. J. F—x.

† I don't trouble myfelf to compare this ftatement with any printed Speech. I put it faithfully as I heard it from his mouth.

" to

" of looking up to particular lines of public characters,
" to whom we may wish the power of the Country to be
" committed." I need not change the words, they are
plain enough of themselves to say, that then the existence
of a party, and the attention of the People to that party,
will be more important than ever. This is a trial indeed
on the common sense of mankind, to which nothing less
than an uncommon preparation of character can be competent. What! when the People are become the real
and effectual spring of that share of power which belongs
to them, must the issue be, and must they have that issue
in contemplation, to commit it again to other hands, to
look up to a party, for it's security? When they shall
have rescued their own compleat check in the Constitution from it's oppression, is it but to surrender it again,
that it may be once more weakened, if not lost? When
they have recovered their Rights, is it needful to look
out for those, who by the encouragement of a strong confidence may abuse or swallow up those Rights again?
Yet, let me pause. The Hon. Gentleman is right. It
is needful for the giving to *Party* a chance of recovering,
under a reform, the influence which it has possessed, that
he should persuade the People to treasure up a *confidence.*
But it is too much to think of answering seriously such an
argument, though from the mouth of that Gentleman;
and quite unnecessary for me, after the pages that are
passed. Either it is answered compleatly, or I must be
ashamed of what I have written. There is an idea in it,
however, which, for the modesty wherein it is couched,
deserves some thanks from a People sensible of what is
due to them; for it expresses, with some indirectness,
what another distinguished advocate* for Aristocratic

* Mr. B—e.

party

party hath made the subject of frequent declarations in the plainest terms, " that the people are not fit to be " trusted with their rights."

The mention of this Gentleman puts me in mind, that he has also, in a very extraordinary publication * some years ago, worked up this argument with laboured inge- nuity. He would give it an air of popularity, by dwell- ing on the flattering idea of consulting the public pleasure in the public appointments. How much the executive power of the Constitution is obliged to him, I leave to another place. But both of them assume for their foun- dation, and evidently in no slender assurance of their party profiting by it, that there are particular lines of public characters exclusively established in the confidence of the country. Most certainly this is an equivocal and divided argument. The late resignations of those gentle- men have by no means confirmed it. Not one despon- dent countenance, but many displeased ones, have those resignations produced in the country. Nor hath the ge- neral contentment with the present Administration of Go- vernment introduced more credit to the argument. Ap- pearances are therefore most certainly against it at pre- sent, and in a moment that must be allowed to carry no small trial with it, and consequently to give no slight ground for judging of the issue in future. That issue, we are inclined to believe, will every day manifest itself more and more in a predilection for those men, whom the People shall behold most direct in the support and recovery of those essential Rights, which are at this time understood and valued too well for any names or con- nexions to think of substituting any other thing in their

* And to similar matter in a Pamphlet en- titled *Thoughts on Discontents*.

* Thoughts on Discontents, p. 41—47.

Read,

ftead, as a capture of the public opinion, or a ground
of it's confidence. With refpect to the mifchiefs, which
Mr. B—e would infinuate, as flowing from the adoption
of other Minifters than thofe who may fancy themfelves
thus pufhed forward by the voice of the Country, this argument is already anfwered; that if they are obnoxious
to the People, the proof will foon appear in a Parliament, which really reprefents the People; and the
cure of the evil will appear too in the difmiffion which
cannot but follow the remonftrances of fuch a Parliament.

But it is fufficient that the Gentleman, firft referred to,
hath announced himfelf, by the whole of this argument
in the hearing of his Electors, the decided Advocate of
a *Party*. Hear it and record it, ye Electors! Hear it, ye
People, throughout the kingdom! Know what is to be
the confequence of the Reform, for which your expectations are on tip-toe. *Publifh it in* Gath, *tell it in the ftreets
of* Afcalon, that THE MAN OF THE PEOPLE IS THE
MAN OF A PARTY—that He, who fighting by your
fide, animated by your favor, and fupported by your
ftrength not lefs than his own, helped to rout the enemies of your freedom, did but rout them to plant the
laurels on the brows of a *Faction*—that when your
ftruggles fhall have fucceeded to place you in the confpicuous exercife of your own natural power, it is his deftination that you fhould ftill be covered in fhade, by thofe
that have uniformly eclipfed your importance.

CHAP.

C H A P. V.

Second Advantage *that will refult from a reformed Reprefentation:* THE CROWN *reftored to it's conftitutional Action.*

The due Prerogatives of the Crown to be valued and cherifhed — the fpecific importance of the regal power —this underwent a revolution in 1688—Independence, the great original principle of the regal power— this evidenced by great antiquity in it's controul over the Parliamentary branches—in it's controul over the orders of Subject's by Rights yet fubfifting—but efpecially in the royal demefnes, the original provifion for the Crown—much dependance introduced by a Civil-Lift-Support. Advantage taken of the Crown under this change by Party —the influence of Party on the executive Power, in it's operations at large—in the appointment to offices of State—hence the influence of a Miniftry fubftituted for that of the Crown, in the enforcement of it's own meafures —how far the fpirit of true Whigifm is concerned in thefe effects—high time that the true friends of the Conftitution fhould be diftinguifhed from Republican Whigs— The application: A reform of Parliamentary Reprefentation the natural cure of thefe wrongs—Independency reftored to one Eftate muft be followed by independency to another, or there is no balance—the royal negative muft confequently feel itfelf in force—an Addrefs to the Crown.

A NOTHER advantage, to which we fhall now fpeak, arifing from a conftitutional correction of parliamentary Reprefentation, will be, that it will furnifh the means of lifting the Crown into it's proper place.

The due prerogatives of the Crown to be valued and cherished.

If any man is actuated by a spirit of narrowing the power of the Crown at all events, if he wishes to diminish an iota of it's due prerogatives, he either knows not the Constitution of his Country, or he is no friend to it. It is natural for mankind, in an abstract view, to look with partiality on the advantages, which aggrandize themselves or their own class. It is too common to feel the impressions of invidious prejudice against those which give others a dominion over them. But for an Englishman to carry these ideas into the system of his own government, betrays not only a narrowness, but a most shameful ignorance, of mind. We ought to know that in the prerogatives, by which others are elevated apparently at the expence of our own enjoyments, the interest we ourselves have is not the least. The full security of all we value most, and the best effect of the powers reserved to our own condition, are consulted even previous to the aggrandizement of those who are thus obnoxious to our minds. Therefore every well-informed Englishman, though he may still dread, as in wisdom he should be taught ever to dread, the power of the Crown, will yet never cease to love it; will cherish it as a very important part of the Constitution under which he feels himself happy, and will support every prerogative that is given it with the same zeal as he would maintain the first personal interest of his own.

The specific importance of the regal Power.

A just affection for the executive branch of the State will never be diminished, where there is a just idea of it's importance. This rests, by the wisdom of ages, in the hands of the Crown, as the great bond of all Power in this Country. The Crown is the key-stone that keeps the whole arch together. It is that *unique* self-existent power in the State, without which the whole legislative branch would be subject, in a variety of circumstances, to very

sensible

senfible and grievous imperfections. It is that vigorous arm of power, which gives force to the whole juftice of **the** Country, and fills the laws with their effect. It is at the fame time that exalted authority, which gives the Country all her weight abroad, and keeps other nations awake to the confideration which is due to the rank fhe bears. It is that fupreme controul, which at home can happily annihilate any of thofe factions, that have rent moft other Governments afunder, and ride fecure amidft a ftorm which can never rife to any danger, where the royal authority is the univerfal counterpoife of all. On the neceffary extent of it's prerogatives we need not look with complaint; when we recollect that their extent hath proved, in the iffue, more beneficial to our liberties than to their owner, and that they are a conftant call on our vigilance to watch for thofe liberties. And we have need to reckon as a bleffing the unalienable indivifibility, with which thofe prerogatives reft on the royal Head; as from this quality, effentially fecured by the Conftitution, the great bond and cement of all, refting in the executive power, can never be diffolved, nor funk into any other branch. Subjects, however afpiring, muft ftill be Subjects: And parts of Government ftanding ever fo high, amidft ever fuch unhappy convulfions, muft in vain expect by this additional grafp to amplify their greatnefs.

As the People of *England* became more enlightened, and confequently more tender, on the fubject of freedom; as, on the other hand, the fyftem of Prerogative eftablifhed in earlier times became more fenfibly grievous to minds improving fo rapidly; a meafure of both prerogative and freedom was at length wifely compounded, fo as to come nearer to the views which later ages had conceived of a

This underwent a reformation in 1688.

more

more balanced Government. This was truly a REVO-
LUTION, important to the Country. If it abridged the
Prince in his power, it made him compenſation in his
happineſs, by ſtrengthening the concord between him and
his People, and bringing the prerogatives that were left
him into a more pointed view, as ſalutary to the exiſtence and the beſt effects of every other power in the
Country.

*Independance,
the great origi-
nal principle of
the regal
power.*

Yet it cannot be amiſs, through the medium of antiquity, to ſee the great principle which the Conſtitution
originally had, and which evermore muſt be kept, in
view as the foundation of royal prerogative, and attached
to all the ſpecies of it's exerciſe. This principle evidently appears to be, *an Independance of the Crown
within it's own Eſtate*, though that Eſtate be circumſcribed
by limits. It is almoſt a reproach to common underſtand-
ing, to ſuppoſe a political ſyſtem of combined powers,
without perfect independance in the limits of each, if
that Government ſo combined is to carry either permanence or authority. Yet there are certain notions concerning the general origin of power (perhaps abſtractly
true, but wrongly applied here, if ſo they ſhould be) and
certain particular circumſtances concerning the maintenance of the Crown in *England*, which may inſinuate to
ſome minds what otherwiſe would not have been ſuppoſed,
and give doubts of that royal Independance, which otherwiſe our firſt reaſonings would concede. Let us therefore
beſtow a little further conſideration on the matter.

In this inquiry I ſhall not take my illuſtrations from the
moſt ancient Conſtitution which our Hiſtory affords, when
neither the Barons nor the People had any regular authority, but the Government was veſted almoſt wholly in the
King;

King; nor from the moſt rigid ſubjects of the prerogative, which even in much later days lifted the *Tudors*
beyond all their predeceſſors. There is no need of going,
for the innocent concluſion I have in view, to times ſo
priſtine, or to evidences ſo **obnoxious**; though, **for the**
uſe to which they **are** adduced, any ſpecies of the latter
may ſurely be inoffenſively ſurveyed.

Nothing **can be more clear, than that for a courſe of** This evidence
many generations from the firſt inſtitution of *Engliſh* by great anti-
legiſlature, the controul of the Crown over the other quity in it's
controul over
branches of it was great—great, **I** mean to ſay; not only the Parliamen
in all the *externals* of the parliamentary function, but in tary branches.
ſome of it's moſt important *internal* movements. I ſhall
hint only to circumſtances which come under the firſt
ſpecies of **controul. The prerogatives of calling the**
legiſlative branches into **exerciſe**, and making their exerciſe, nay, the very Being **of one** of them, to ceaſe, are
alone ſufficient demonſtrations **of an** independant power
in him that can do theſe acts. In addition to which, modern uſage **hath preſerved other memorials of** the ſame
power, **in** the requeſt which the Commons make to the
Crown, at the commencement of every new Parliament,
for leave **to chuſe a Speaker, and** to enjoy their wonted
privileges.

If ſo **much appears with** reſpect **to** the legiſlative body, In it's controul
we may **expect** more numerous manifeſtations **of** the over the order
of ſubjects, b
high independance of the Crown in it's controul over all Rights yet ſub
orders of it's ſubjects, **and** their general affairs. Let the ſiſting.
powers, which grew **out of the** feudal law, periſh **with**
their ſource. Yet thus far let it be remembered, that
this feudal ſyſtem was brought into this kingdom by the
ſame monarch who introduced the greater outlines of our

present government; that the evidence it gave of a natural independance in the Crown still speaks in reason; and that when it was abolished, being abolished by compact with the Crown, neither could the abolition reach, nor could the crown intend it to reach, to the extinction of that original sovereign spirit, with which, even by means of this system among others, it presided in the Constitution. To this moment the same supremacy of judicial sentence, which anciently passed from the King himself *in his Court* in all causes of his people, civil and criminal, is supposed and acknowledged to abide in him, and to pass from him, by the forms of the Courts into which the all-comprehensive judicature of *the King's* ancient *Court* is distributed. The doctrine of Escheats to the Crown for crimes, and for default of heirs, still subsisting, announces in the plainest manner the idea conceived by our forefathers of a superior independant controul over property, and that the primary notion of it's being a *beneficiary* possession has never yet been entirely lost.

But especially in the royal demesnes, the original provision for the Crown.

But we would rather dwell on what is direct and self-evident in it's nature, and which no possibility of argument can evade : I mean, the royal demesnes. These were originally and for many centuries very extensive, and comprehended, besides a great number of manors, most part of the chief cities in the kingdom. This is the manner in which the Constitution intended to provide for the royal branch of the Government. It was not in the nature of things for an independant indefeasible Estate to be erected on a more solid ground—a permanence of hereditary property vested in those hands, unto which, as paramount every other, all other property might by contingency escheat, itself incapable of escheat or loss.

lofs. Whether this allotment of power had it's origin from the People, or from the self-appropriating hand of the conquering Norman, is not material; it is the great plan of the Conſtitution, ſanctioned by ages. And that duration might never fail the independency which was thus given to the royal Eſtate, it was eſtabliſhed by law* that the King could alienate no part of his demeſnes, and that he himſelf or his ſucceſſors might at any time reſume ſuch donations. That law indeed was but irregularly obſerved; and from thence flowed more ſerious conſequences than were apprehended at the time, or perhaps have ſince been properly recollected. The flattering figures of a high Civil Liſt but poorly compenſate for invading that fixed inheritance, which hath enabled many other monarchs to riſe ſuperior to aſſailing ſtorms, when other reliances have crumbled beneath them; if indeed thoſe flattering figures do compenſate, in fact, for the more ſolid intereſts whoſe value they ſeem to have obſcured. Let me not be miſtaken. I mean not to ſpeak of that fixed inheritance, as wiſhing it poſſible that it could revert, or to ſay that the ſyſtem of the Civil Liſt is not a better ſyſtem for the People. I produce the former merely for the conſtitutional principle it brings in this queſtion. And, beyond a doubt, the moment thoſe alienations took place, a door was opened for throwing a ſhade over the natural brilliancy which was given to the royal Eſtate. At leaſt, the unfavorable idea of dependance came in with the acceptance of a proviſion from the Commons: While it is certain that the Crown, being found vulnerable in this quarter, notwithſtanding that proviſion is ſettled for life, has ſuſtained many trying

Much dependance introduced by a Civil Liſt ſupport.

* Fleta, lib. 1. cap. 8. § 17. lib. 3. cap. 6. § 3. Bracton, lib. 2. cap. 5.

aſſaults

assaults from Faction, which would never have been made, had it rested immoveable on it's first foundation.

We must prosecute this thought farther, because it will bring us to our point. How inextinguishable soever, notwithstanding these alterations in the royal revenue, the great principle remains of a most perfect independance in the Crown, certainly advantage hath been taken of the change. And by whom? By that Party, or, what is the same thing, by those who have ever acted on the same principles with that Party, which having made itself strong in parliamentary interest, hath ever been most watchful to keep and increase it's power—watchful to profit by those diminutions which popular Rights have at any time sustained, or by those circumstances which, embarrassing the actions of the Crown, have at any time made it more easily tangible by it's subjects. The bare notion of Dependance is to some minds a *stimulus* of invasion. And in every struggle of a public nature for more than a century past, the Crown hath in some measure experienced this invasion. Whatever may have been gained by other powers, this hath certainly been no solid gainer on the whole. Let the object be what it might, all seemed perfectly contented, if the Crown from it's plenitude made up the deficiency that was any where felt. And how should not any issue terminate in it's loss, where there was a compact in the Country ready to direct all public contingences to it's prejudice? In every disposition of Power which marks the royal government, or even the royal pleasure, the Crown hath felt the weights with which the hands of such a party have clogged it—it's nerves have actually become unstrung.

Advantage taken of the Crown under this change, by Party.

What

What is become of the executive power of the Constitution? If this, in it's very outset, is merely nominal in the Crown, it's arm has, by the grasp of Party, been certainly rendered feeble in it's whole operations. How should this be otherwise? For the first thing looked for by a Party in the execution of measures is not the men most competent to the occasion, but the men most true to their connexion. Thus the executive branch has not unfrequently been made an absolute sacrifice not to wrong designs, but to an unhappy favouritism of attachment or opinion. But suppose such a Party possessed of no actual administration of the Country, yet if it lies in wait to cavil and molest, it may injure the executive power as much by damping it's vigour, as by absorbing the whole of it's original direction. Under the menace of such a Party, how can the *salus populi* employ the free efforts of the executive branch? It's best measures have travelled but a short way towards their end, before they feel themselves spent; the good, that was meditated, is rendered abortive; the evil, which called up vigour to extinguish it, gains strength by the temporary sufferance at least, which intrigue has rendered difficult to be shunned; inquiry is stifled; punishment cannot find it's way; abuses look with triumph over the eye that sees them: In the mean time, all that are disappointed, all that have done wrong, need but seek the wing of such a Party, and they will find within it a protection, which shall either repel every shaft of Power, or greatly blunt it's edge.

But let us ask another question. The appointment to all the offices in the State—is the Crown as free in this as it was meant to be? Can any man be ignorant how untowardly this prerogative hath been treated by the grasp of Party? Is there a private Gentleman in the Country,

The influence of Party on the executive Power, in it's whole operations.

In appointment to the offices of State.

Country, who does not exercise with more unrestricted freedom the appointment of his servants, and the general diftributions of his power, than the prince under whom he lives? Is there a king on the throne of the *Mahrattas*, furrounded by all his, dictating nobles, who cannot render to his own perfonal defires more abundant indulgences from this branch of royal authority? I allow there are cafes, where the public affections may be ftrongly interested. And the public voice will ever be attended to by the genuin Father of his People, whofe Government moves on proper principles. The very intention of all prerogative was to facilitate the public happinefs. But, let not every endeavor of combined individuals to force themfelves into the royal clofet, though backed by fome fhare of popular opinion, be confidered as a fit cafe to wreft from the monarch the confidence, which is as precious to his breaft as to another man's. Thofe cafes are fo ftrongly characterized, where they rife, as not eafily to be miftaken. And were the Parliament brought to be a real Reprefentative of the People, the Crown would never fail to know them from it's voice, at once the moft fatisfactory conveyance of the fenfe of the People, and their beft ground of reliance that no finifter councils can long deprive their fenfe of it's natural impreffion on the royal mind.

Hence the influence of a miniftry fubftituted for that of the Crown, in the enforcement of it's own meafures.

But once more. Where is the perfonal influence of the Crown, which fhould naturally give weight and authority to it's own meafures? The Crown hath, in truth, been taught a very different experience from what this language would convey. It is not it's own natural authority, but the weight of a Miniftry extenfive in it's connexions, and powerful in Parliament, that fhall give facility and effect to the whole executive power. Is this

the

the language of the Conftitution? But is it not the fact; experienced, with very little interruption, by every prince that hath filled this throne, from the arrival of the glorious Deliverer, *William* III? And was the Crown left by our forefathers, in the narroweft days it has feen, fo feeble and unimportant as to be indebted for all it's public effect to the adventitious fuccors of it's own fervants? A Republican may embrace the idea, but a conftitutional Englifhman will renounce it.

" You will reply, " that to fimplify thus the power of
" the Crown, by bringing it's own acts to itfelf, and com-
" preffing it's authority within it's own circle, is not the
" principle of Whigs. It is a maxim of theirs to mode-
" rate and let down the fpecific power of the Crown,
" by blending in it's movements fuch a mixture of the
" public weight, as to lofe much of prerogative in the
" popular caft." I grant this is a principle of Whigs.
But of what Whigs? Of Whigs connected in a Party,
and pledged to the aggrandifement of that Party. With
fuch it is of importance, not merely that the fpecific
virtue of unqueftionable prerogative fhould be abated,
but that while the democratic name gathers what the
Crown thus lofes, the power thus gained fhall in fact reft
with themfelves. I know of no principles in the code of
pure independent Whigifm, that emulate to defraud the
Crown of the full virtue and original brilliancy of it's
own conftitutional authority : this Whiggifm is fatisfied,
if the regal authority keeps within it's conftitutional
limits. But the other is Whiggifm in it's phrenfy. Nay, it
is more. It is downright the republican fpirit. For it
will not only introduce more heads into the Government,
but every head introduced is directly fubverfive of the
monarchic.

[marginal note: How far the fpirit of true Whiggifm is concerned in thefe effects.]

M   Let

igh time that
ie friends of
ie Constitution
hould be dif-
inguished from
Republican
Whigs.

Let those who, affecting to befriend the interests of the public, approve the maxims of such a system, take to themselves and avow at once the denomination which befits them ; but let honest men, who mean no such things, stand free from the imputation. It is high time the distinction should be made and understood, that the friends of the people may be rescued from the misconstruction, which the peculiar views of a few may have fastened on a greater number ; or, if the number be smaller, that they may be known for what they are. They are friends of the People : but they are equal friends to the Crown, because they are friends to the whole Constitution. They are friends to it on the most perfect independence of all it's parts. But they are not Republicans : They will no more part with an iota of the monarchy, or it's established prerogatives, than with an article of *Magna Charta*, or *the Bill of Rights*. Neither are they friends to *Party*. For Party will level all boundaries to enlarge it's own. It may assume the more inoffensive name of *Connexion :* and connexions are honorable, when they do not thrive by depredation on others. It may plead to be *useful*, as a combined power is stronger than a single one : and the plea would have merit, if any other than itself was in prospect to be served. It is convenient indeed for *weak* men, who have not abilities to figure by themselves ; or for *bad* men, who may wish to hide, or to strengthen, the views of their abilities by the group of numbers. But it hath been the curse of every Government that hath known it : and the public good of *England*, as well as the honour and efficiency of her Crown, have not less than any others to complain of at it's hands.

he Applica-
on.

We will now hasten to the Conclusion for which we have been preparing. The view we have
had

had of the advantage which has been taken of the Crown, and particularly within the prefent century, was needful to fhew how widely the defects of parliamentary Reprefentation have fpread themfelves, having laid the foundation for thofe partial abforptions of political interefts, which have held all the parts of the Conftitution in a degree of bondage. It was needful, by pointing to the original fource of the diforder, and marking it's progrefs, to fhew whence the remedy muft proceed, and of what nature it muft be. So long as Factions powerful in Parliament, and of courfe largely controuling the independency of that Affembly, can maintain their footing there, the Crown muft expect to be held at bay, and to endure thofe diminutions of it's independence, which it has been taught to experience. Let the Reprefentatives be reftored to *their* independent purity, and the cure effected there will reach to every other wound, by which any other part of the Conftitution has been maimed. It muft reach every other in the nature of things, by the inevitable fympathy with which all the parts of the political, as well as the natural, body never ceafe to be mutually affected by what gives health or injury to each. The Crown will feel the reftoration of it's own powers in the moft demonftrative manner. Remove the weight that keeps down a fpring, and it will inftantly fly into it's priftine action.

A reform of parliamentary Reprefentation the natural cure of thefe wrongs.

But independency reftored to one of the three Eftates muft be followed in wifdom, if it could fail in the fpontaneous nature of things, by equal independence to the other two. As three concordant checks, they muft all be brought to an equal bearing, they muft all be ftrung to a perfect tone. The inftrument that is relaxed but in one of it's chords, grates upon the ear in difcord. The drum of war, if left unbraced, or but unequally

Independency reftored to one Eftate, muft be followed by independency in another, or there is no balance.

braced

braced, in a fingle fpace, gives not the found which calls the foldier up, and bids him take his heedful ftand on duty. Not lefs difcordant, hollow, and unnatural will be the Government, intended as ours to fpring from a three-fold harmony of parts, if all do not act with equal force upon the fyftem. Suppofe the Houfe of Commons was fet firm and upright on it's own natural column, the mafs of the People. Care muft be taken, if there fhould be need, that the Crown fhould alfo feel itfelf erect and ftrong on it's own bafe; elfe the edifice would over-fet from the inequality of it's fupports: the Commons would be an overmatch for the Prince. The difadvan-tage to the Crown, unhappily too long accuftomed to be viewed in oppofition to the whole People, and narrowed befides in all it's exercife by combinations within the po-pular body, would long ago have come to a crifis fore and fatal to it, if in the general diforders of all the con-ftitutional branches it had not obtained fome counter-balance over the Commons, by a portion of influence which a melioration of their virtue will fpeedily annihi-late. Suppofe, on the other hand, the Crown was re-ftored to it's natural felf-exiftent action, without a pro-portionable lift to the independency of the Commons: we may eafily conceive, from what ftand the former is now enabled to make againft a general tendency in the latter to reduce it, what chance would then be left to popular free-dom, perhaps betrayed by it's own combinations, and born down by another power beyond it's refiftance. It is therefore beft, perhaps, if diforder muft invade the Go-vernment, that it run pretty equally through all the branches, thus faving all by the debility which leaves each nearly on a level ftill. But a balance in ill is the moft wretched of confolations. Let us look to a balance of good. The Conftitution plainly intended fuch a

balance

balance in the formation of it's Estates. Such a balance can alone be the emulation of every wise reformer. And the means, the hour too, are now before us to see it properly established.

While we are speaking of this constitutional balance, and especially as it will shew itself in the Crown, it is impossible not to observe, that when once the independency of the Commons shall be restored, it will be proper that whatever check the Crown is possessed of by it's negative, over the other branches of the legislature, should be brought into it's natural force. The self-evident nature of the prerogative I now allude to, one would think, might have spared it from ever being made the subject of a problem. But as a Right Hon. Gentleman *, who has already been mentioned, has thought fit on a late occasion to bring a heavy invective against this idea, this will induce me to make some reflexions on the matter, which without such a call for them, I should fear, would have subjected me to the imputation of contending, like a *Quixote*, with imaginary windmills.

The regal negative must consequently feel itself in force.

The negative of the Crown, or it's Right of rejecting what Parliament has agreed to, is the great and essential circumstance, by which it holds that important branch of it's independence, it's share in the legislature. No greater right than this it can have consistent with general liberty, or even with any rational system of legislation. Were the King to have the power of *resolving*, his influence on the Supplies, to name no other matters, would be so great, that the theoretical absurdity of his giving and granting to himself would be the least evil; the People

---

* Mr. F—x, in his Speech to the Electors of *Westminster*, 17th July 1782.

granting

would feel in reality, and with a foreness not eafily
endured, that he took the money out of their own
pockets. But a right of rejecting he has, becaufe without this he has nothing——nothing to leave his own prerogatives in fafety for an hour. Now when can it be fo
proper that this negative fhould be brought forward into
fight, as when Parliament has recovered that original independence, which gives it's full controul in the Government ? If what we have often heard from the Honorable
Gentleman abovementioned be true, that the influence
of the Crown fo far pervades the two Houfes of Parliament, as to hold them at it's pleafure; this is a reafon
why the royal negative now fleeps, and has for fometime flept, in fuch a flate of things. There can be no
room for it, where all things move at the monarch's pleafure, or can be moulded to produce it. But change this
flate of things, and the reafon affecting this prerogative
becomes changed at the fame moment. The Crown muft
then take a different ground, fhould the views of Parliament differ materially from it's own, to preferve it's balance.
Is Parliament free and uncontrouled in it's procedure? This
legiflative fhare in the Crown muft feel itfelf equally free
and uncontrouled. It muft be fo, or the Crown muft be at
the mercy of the two Houfes. A mutual independence
calls for a mutual unrefervednefs of diffent. And if ever
this be needful to be exercifed at one time more than another (it is impoffible I fhould be underftood to mean, *un-
reafonably and wantonly* exercifed, but *more freely* than
perhaps for long periods may have been done, *as freely* as
either Houfe of Parliament exercifes it towards the other)
it is furely when it is become again the main check that
is left to the Crown ; unlefs the regal privileges are to
vanifh into names and fhadows, while thofe of the other
Eftates remain in all their pointed effect.

But

But this is a folid prerogative; immoveable, if the Conftitution is to ftand. To inveigh againft the exercife of it at any time, in the full difcretion of the Crown, is the heighth of political phrenzy. Comparatively fpeaking, it is of more confequence that the legiflative Power fhould be under a decided and inftant check, than the executive : For the encroachments, which the latter can only effect by a train of artful meafures, the former may accomplifh in a moment. And the check that is thus given to it ought, for thefe reafons, to be kept in view, as oft as fit occafions prefent themfelves. It is by the infrequency of it's exercife that not only offence [*] grows up, which elfe would never have been taken, but the important diftinctions of Power become gradually loft in confufion, through the impreffions of this offence on the one hand, and the affumptions which it gathers to itfelf on the other. Suppofe the two Houfes of Parliament fhould trench inordinately on any public or private Rights; fhould agree to take away the eftate of an individual, to difpofe improvidently of public interefts, to unhinge any barriers of the State, to take away the King's Civil Lift, or reduce it extremely, or to pafs any other bills of an intemperate nature; fhall not the Crown judge for itfelf of thefe meafures, and fhall it be matter of more offence that it pronounces the abfolute *veto*, with which the Conftitution hath armed it, than we ever find to have been taken by one Houfe to the other's rejection of its Refolves? Thefe cafes are by no means too extravagant for fuppofition, becaufe they are

---

[*] The rejecting a bill (fays *Bifhop Burnet*) though an unqueftionable Right of the Crown, has been fo feldom practifed, that the two Houfes are apt to think it a hardfhip, when there is a bill denied. *Burnet's Own Time Vol. III. p. 140.*

not more extravagant than have been experienced. The
Commons, before now, have voted away the Houſe of
Peers, have voted the excluſion of the immediate heir to
the Crown, have voted the deſtruction of the Monarch
himſelf. The Lords have voted the eſtabliſhment of
compleat paſſive obedience; and again, on the other
hand, they have voted, at one time or other, the moſt
formidable attacks on various branches of acknowledged
Prerogative. And both together have concurred in
bills, ſometimes rejected by the Crown, and ſometimes
not, very cenſurably infringing on the true ſpirit of
the Conſtitution. And much more likely are reſolves
of a ſtriding nature to take place, when the legiſlative
Aſſembly ſhall feel itſelf ſtrong in freedom; and eſpecially that part of it which repreſents democratic
ſway.

It is curious to ſee how ſtrangely ſome men reaſon on
this ſubject. In caſes as ſtrongly marked as thoſe above-
mentioned, but eſpecially in all caſes which tend to di-
miniſh the democratic influence, they are ready to call
aloud for the exertion of this prerogative. On the *Septennial Bill* it has been ſaid over and over, that King
George I. ſhould have interpoſed his negative, and with
more tenaciouſneſs than it found in King *William* III.
upon the *Triennial*. But in caſes wherein the Country
might perhaps feel itſelf gratified at ſome expence to
the regal power, or in caſes of general legiſlation, it is
pronounced by the ſame perſons inſufferable, ſhould
the Crown expreſs it's diſſent to the majority of Parliament, though perhaps that majority has before met in
it's progreſs the diſſent of very numerous and very re-
ſpectable characters in both Houſes. The queſtion
therefore comes to be aſked, by whoſe judgment, and at
whoſe

whofe pleafure, is this royal negative to be directed ? By the King's own feelings, in a power abfolutely lodged with himfelf? Or by the People, or any portions of the People, over whofe power that negative was placed as a check? Nay, the queftion will be, whether this be a power with any reality ? It is a real and effective prerogative, or it is not. If it is not, then let us no longer abufe common fenfe, by calling and petitioning for it's interpofition, though the Conftitution and the firft privileges of the People may by that interpofition be faved. If it is a prorogative with real power, then is it equally abhorrent from common fenfe to introduce any other arbiter of it's exercife than the difcretion of him, whofe prerogative it is. Efpecially if we reflect further,

What mifchief can ever arife from the royal Negative, were it even capricioufly and frequently exercifed ? The Parliament, on behalf of themfelves and the Country, are poffeffed of an effectual counterbalance. They hold the public purfe ; from their hands the Crown now derives its fupplies ; and though the immediate Civil Lift, being fettled for life, might not be affected by any difpleafure they took, yet there are various other heads of fupplies, important not only to the fatisfaction of the Crown, but to great purpofes of Government, by the detention of which the executive Power would be confiderably embarraffed. Thefe have from very ancient times been frequently detained on any occafions of difcontent. The check therefore over the royal Negative is at all times a moft important one. With this in profpect, and efpecially in the hands of an independent Parliament, the Monarch will duly confider before he interpofes this

N   prerogative :

prerogative : And should he do it with much dissatisfac-
tion to Parliament, the means of producing more
deliberate reviews of the matter are the strongest
that wisdom can devise. But then the stronger and
the freer this check, in the nature of it, is in the
hands of Parliament, and especially of an independent one, the more perfectly free should be the use of
this Prerogative in the hands of the Crown, and with
such a Parliament. Indeed, comparing the nature of the
two checks together, the advantage after all preponderates greatly in favor of Parliament : To say the truth,
it preponderates on that side too much, to leave the
royal Negative perfectly independent. While the Crown,
to back it's own prerogative, has no consequences, which
it can bring home to the *feelings* of Parliament, equally
forcible with what it runs the risque of meeting from
them, the Hon. Gentleman abovementioned may surely
have the charity to leave it to the freest exercise of what
powers are given it, inferior as they are, and unequal to
the resistance that is provided against them.

He seems to think it strengthens his objections, " that
" near a century has passed without an instance in which
" this prerogative has been exerted." To draw a precedent from the forbearance of a right against that right
itself, is not the argument of a very ingenuous mind ; and
will have less weight here, when we look back to the
cause before alluded to, as insisted on by the Hon. Gentleman himself, why the exertion of this prerogative has
for a series of time been rendered needless. But let
him reflect in what reign those instances last occurred,
and if he be true to his friends, his objections must sink
in silence. Does this new ally of Whigs mean covertly

to

to brand the memory of *Will.* III.? Did that mildest of Princes exert a prerogative, which shall become the subject of invective in the mouth even of him that would seem to associate with Whigs? Shall it be insinuated, that any other Monarch on the English Throne, acting on the principles of that great Deliverer, shall become inordinate in his measures?

In this question, I know, artful demagogues may practise greatly on the jealousy of a People, unless they are sufficiently dispassionate to see the true situation of the case. Appealing to my countrymen, I would put that true situation of the case thus briefly before them, " Are you willing that the Crown should retain an un- " natural and corrupt influence over Parliament, or the " natural and salutary interference which belongs to it ? " One or the other, in the nature of things, it *must* " have, it *will* have, and I do not hesitate to say, it " *should* have, if a Crown is to remain in the Country. " Let us grant then that it now has the former in any " degree : The more zealous should you be to exchange " it for the latter. Have you profited by the substitution " of the unnatural for the natural controul ? Can you then " possibly suffer by the re-exchange ? That re-exchange " will make you feel a tone of power, to which you " have long been strangers. And if it gives an equal " tone to the power of another, you are more equal to " cope with that power in your natural strength than in " your weakness."

Were I sure that these sheets would have the honor of making their **way** into the hands of our illustrious Sovereign, reverting to the object of my arguments, in which the regal Estate bears so distinguished a concern, I would

N 2   indulge

indulge myfelf, before I clofe what relates to that Eftate, in an humble but moft fincere Addrefs to the royal feelings on this important fubject. But taking my chance for what may happen, my own duty will not be fatisfied without touching, in fome few words, what involves his intereft as the monarch of a free and manly nation. I would fay : if the Sovereign would render his name immortal, now is the moment before him. For, doubtlefs, we muft facrifice what we know to what we might wifh, fhould we deny that much of the ability to effect this glorious reform will come with the greateft facility from the royal encouragement. To reftore the relaxed powers of a free Conftitution, to give new finews to a People, to emerge from the corrupt means of ambition into a manly fyftem of free and generous rule, is an heroifm unknown to thofe who have filled the thrones of modern empires. Antiquity muft fail in the paralel : for to found kingdoms, and bring forward a People, in original freedom falls infinitely fhort, as it is making no facrifice of any thing which the habits of enjoyment and tafted temptation have rendered dear. The Prince, who can evacuate his heart and his hands of all that has long filled both at the expence of much freedom and happinefs to his People, may claim the enthufiafm of the hiftoric page.

Have years of difcontent rolled on? Here they will, obtain a moft delightful oblivion. They will be cancelled by a happinefs, that will make the moft liberal amends. The People will even welcome the recollection of thofe ills, which have worked their own cure, and brought forth in the iffue a Patriot King!

Have paft prejudices on the Rights of Government found their way into the royal mind? What man more
abroad

abroad in the world to difcufs and meafure prejudices, has not felt their contracting influence? But to conquer them is the difficulty, which has been more rarely paffed in any conditions of life. In a Prince, this is the completion of the human underftanding;—in a Prince, who can blend with that conqueft an emulation to fee his People free in the meafure of their own movements, and vigorous in the fatisfaction of that freedom. His Majefty has therefore before him what fhould ever be dear to the ambition of ever crowned Head, the manifeftation of a mind uncommonly enlightened to all the views of genuin greatnefs—a mind capable, in very trying circumftances, of leaving the generality of mankind as much below the reach to which it can ftretch itfelf, as they are below the ftation which it fills.

As perfonal to his own happinefs, no lefs than to his own glory, the foundeft policy will invite the Sovereign to the meafure before us. To throw down whatever proudly erects itfelf between him and his People, only to create jealoufies in both, to derange the natural union of both, and to obfcure both to the views of each, muft earneftly be coveted by wifdom. To keep up his People in the full importance which the free principles of the State have given them, is to fecure to himfelf, and all that fucceed him in that plan of Government, an eftablifhment in their hearts. A free nation, a nation freely treated, is a generous nation; their obedience is the ftedfaftnefs of principle, their affection is a rock. The utmoft wifhes of imperial glory cannot go beyond the Government of fuch a nation. Let the Sovereign then found his kingdom in the true freedom of his people : let him know nothing but his own pure Rights, and their's, in all their mutual vigour : and their affections, compleating the fuperftructure, will provide the cement that will

hold

hold it ftrong for ever. He may bid defiance to Faction and Party : he may fpare himfelf the labour of intrigues : while his own prerogatives will fecurely maintain him in the juft affertion of his rule, the love and confidence of his fubjects will let him fee the day, when they will make one caufe with Prerogative, to ftrengthen the hands of him who approves himfelf *the Father of his People.*.

Thefe humble fuggeftions we venture the more readily to offer, becaufe one and twenty years ago the mind of the Sovereign, who then fat on the Britifh throne, was known to be animated with the pureft defires to fee his People and the Conftitution, as well as his own So-vereignty, free. In that period the true friend of the Country, the immortal PITT, filled alike the Cabinet and the royal breaft with his falutary counfels. Aufpici-ous æra ! had not the corrupting Dæmon entered. That Prince knew the unworthy bondage, in which his royal Predeceffors, the whole legiflative power, and the rights of the people had been held for near an age—from the time that thofe, who had been fuccefsful in limiting the Government, determined not to lofe the hold they had gained, but thenceforth made Parliament the feat of their power, fettering the Monarch with their hands, and keeping the People under their feet. Not more for him-felf than for the other branches of the Government, that Prince renounced the ignominious and unnatural yoke. His heart was prepared for it's choice, to join the caufe of the People, to emancipate all the parts of the State, and lift them into their due vigour. Here therefore the ob-jects we would prefs gather fome degree of confidence. We wifh but that the fentiments, which have filled the throne, may revert to themfelves again. May the patriot views of 1761, mark the political glory of 1782. This

year

year hath already been diftinguifhed by ineftimable events, which will ever be memorable in the annals of *England* and *Ireland*. May it be crowned with one farther glory— the avowed interpofition of the fovereign, to effect a more equal Reprefentation in Parliament, and to render the Houfe of Commons a real Reprefentative of the People, conformably to the defires of thofe who have earneftly petitioned for this, and to what muft be equally the defire of all his fubjects. Then he may fay with *Horace*, and applauding pofterity will confecrate in un-perifhable annals the *Eulogium* for his own,

  Exegi monumentum ære perennius,
  Regalique fitu pyramidum altius ;
  Quod **non imber** edax, non Aquilo impotens
  Poffit diruere, aut innumerabilis
  Annorum feries, et fuga temporum.
  Non omnis moriar ; multaque pars mei
  Vitabit Libitinam : ufque ego poftera
  Crefcam laude recens.

CHAP. VI.

The DURATION *of Parliament.*

Intimately connected with the subject of Representation—the greatness of delegated power should ever be balanced by it's brevity of duration—by the wisdom of most States the period of a year has been adopted—this the ancient policy of our own Country in the parliamentary Trust—how it came to be varied—partly by the acquiescence of the People in triennial acts—the septennial act the grossest violation of Law, Constitution, and Decency—that act must at all events be done away—how much farther we must go—without short Parliaments no amendment of the Representation can do good.

HITHERTO we have considered our subject in general terms, without coming to any specification of remedy in mode or in extent. We conceive it impossible for a candid mind to survey the evils, with which our unequal Representation is replete, and to be at any great loss where to apply the cure. Men of prudence may differ about the extent to which they should go, but all dispassionate men will agree that to *some* extent they must go, so as effectually to get rid of those more pointed circumstances, from which the evils we complain of originate.

Whether or not the duration of Parliament be considered as forming a question in the subject of unequal Representation, most certainly it is closely connected with Representation in general, and is one of those circumstances of which the eye must be brought to take a very special and considerate view, as a principal source of the

evils

evils we feel. In difcuffing therefore, fo comprehenfively as we have profeffed to do, the important fubject before us, we fhould leave it very imperfectly treated in our own opinion, nay, we fhould leave one of it's moft dangerous circumftances unregarded, were we not to call the attention of our readers, in the moft pointed manner, to the neceffity of a reform in the Duration of Parliament. For if the Reprefentation were at this hour made as perfect as we could wifh it, the duration of the parliamentary truft, continuing as it is, would of itfelf furnifh the means for overfeting all the fecurity of which we might fancy ourfelves poffeffed. We fhall therefore fubjoin a few obfervations on this queftion; and they need but to be few, as the queftion itfelf, in what relates to its conftitution and its policy, lies in a fhort compafs.

It is a principle, whofe foundation can never be fhaken, that the greatnefs of power vefted in any portion of the people, fhould ever be balanced by the brevity of its duration. All the beft governments in the world have fhewn their attention to this idea. By the frequent rotations and fucceffions of authority, factions are moft eafily broken, and abufes of all kinds moft eafily corrected; at leaft thofe, to whom the delegation reverts, have the means, if they will ufe them, of giving new vigour to the purpofes for which the delegation was eftablifhed. There feems not in human wifdom a mean more effectual than this, to keep power within its limits; nor a reafonable profpect, without this, of reftraining the licence, which the enjoyment of power will ever affume. And if the power committed be that of reprefenting others, fpeaking their voices, and managing their interefts; the nature of fuch a truft more efpecially makes it a fhort one, if thofe that give it would have

The greatnefs of delegated power fhould ever be balanced by it's brevity of duration.

O

it

it kept within the bounds of an agency, and not arrive at the assertion of an independent and original function.

By the wisdom of most states the period of a year has been adopted.

In the establishments of such a trust, whether from a whole people, or from any lesser portions of them, the wisdom of mankind has with great uniformity concurred in the expedient of limiting it to the duration of a year. Indeed this policy has been carried in almost all countries, and at all times, to the appointment of magistracies vested with extensive authority. And with respect to these, in some petty republics environed by powerful neighbors, and therefore greatly dependent on the fidelity of those who are in authority, this period of a year has been considerably narrowed. Thus at *Lucca* the magistrates are chosen only for two months. At *Ragusa**** the chief magistrate is changed every month, the other officers every week, and the governor of the castle every day. But these are regulations that neither are called for by powerful states, nor are fit for such. A period shorter than a year is incompetent to the execution of larger interests; and a longer period seems to have been considered by all as dangerous to any interests that have importance to plead.

This the ancient policy of our own country in the parliamentary trust.

In our own country this sentiment has preponderated, in the limitation of all delegated and subordinate authority, as much as in any other. With respect to the parliamentary trust, the highest of our delegated powers, it is not to be disputed, that in its origin it was limited to the duration of a year, and for a long time continued under that limitation. In analogy to this rule various other parts of the government still move. Most

* Tournefort's Voyages.

of

of the magiſtracies in the kingdom, that are elective in their nature, and many popular offices which are not, are determinable at the ſame period. The parliament itſelf, in many of its functions, is guided by the ſame limitation. The national ſupplies are voted only for a year. The national defence, in the army, is provided only for the ſame period. Theſe meaſures keep pace, in their cauſe, with the purpoſe of an annual parliament. If there would be danger in a ſtanding army, there is equal danger in a ſtanding parliament. The ſupplies might be voted without great inconvenience or impropriety, in times of peace, for more years than one; but then, on the principle originally aſſumed, one parliament would be doing the buſineſs of another.

That Parliaments were annual in their inſtitution is therefore unqueſtionable. The ſtatutes of *Edward* III. ordaining that a *Parliament ſhould be held once in every year, and oftener, if need be*, were but declaratory of that paſt uſage, which had become law, and was conſidered as a birth-right. The intention of them was, that not only *a Parliament* ſhould be held every year, but a *new* Parliament; and the writs iſſued in that age, which may yet be conſulted, ſhew that this was not only the principle but the practice. However through an incautiouſneſs of expreſſion room was given, in proceſs of time, for ſuch a conſtruction of thoſe ſtatutes as defeated both thoſe parts of their intention. By coupling the conditional words, *if need be*, with the former clauſe, *once in every year*, as well as with the latter clauſe, *and oftener*, not only *a Seſſion* of Parliament every year was obviated, but much more the neceſſity of a *new* Parliament. And thus the hands of the Monarch, which were clearly intended to be tied, were left perfectly free to ſuch diſcretion alone as

the circumstances of the times might recommend. If
the times were unfavorable to such a latitude of interpretation as this, which introduced an entire frustration of
those statutes, another interpretation was employed, which
equally avoided the idea of a *new* Parliament; on which,
it was urged, those statutes were totally silent, even supposing the former clause abovementioned to be absolute
in it's sense, and the conditional words attached only to
the latter. Yet here we must observe, that the words,
and oftner, seem to us indisputably to involve the idea of
a *new* Parliament. For extremely incongruous must have
been the application of those words to the repeated meet-
ings in the same year of a Parliament which continued the
same: by whatever circumstances it's sitting might be in-
terrupted, certainly it could never be considered as more
than *one* Session—the same Parliament could not be *held
oftner* in the same year; the idea of a dissolution seems
therefore naturally supposed.

On the one or the other of those interpretations above-
mentioned, according as the people were more or less
tenacious on the subject of the parliamentary function,
the executive power took occasion, in a course of time,
to conduct itself in the use of Parliaments: so that either
there was not a constant Session of Parliament every
year, or, when afterwards there was, this was thought
enough to satisfy those acts: nay, a foundation seemed to
be laid for waving the idea of new and frequent Elections;
which instead of gaining ground, lost it so far after a while,
and doubtless through the supineness of the People, as to
feel their return not with the revolution of the year, but
with the demise of the prince. That the regal power,
especially in times when it was less balanced, should give
admission to either of those interpretations, which left it's
own

own hands more free to act, will give furprize to none. That the Reprefentatives themfelves fhould fuffer thofe interpretations to pafs, and not be forward to pufh any affertions of popular rights, which might expedite the extinction of their own political being, is as eafily to be conceived as that any individual will prefer his own enjoyment to the intereft of his country.

But what followed this aftonifhing departure from the fpirit of antiquity in the firft periods of the Houfe of Commons? What fteps did the Country take, when recovering it's fpirit, to recover what was intended to be recorded as it's rights? As if deferting the principle of annual parliaments, nay, and conceding the interpretation which had avoided the neceffity even of an annual feffion, the firft interpofition of the Commons on this queftion was by a bill for *triennial* elections, which fecured only a feffion once in the three years. This was obtained under the unhappy *Charles*, whofe worfe-deferving fon rendered but of fhort duration this approximating ftep towards the eftablifhment of a more regular popular check. We blufh to fay further how this Act came to be repealed, and Parliament thrown again upon the royal difcretion. In another period, however, under *William* III. the Commons, not from hoftility to the prince, but urged by the interefts and the voice of the people, come again with fuccefs to this important claim. In what terms? For an annual feffion indeed, but for no more than a triennial election. And it is remarkable, that while this ftatute recognizes the ancient laws and ftatutes of the realm for new and frequent Parliaments, and pronounces thefe to be falutary both to the King and the People, it is worded as if declaratory in it's provifions

of

of what was confidered to be the Conftitution of the Country.

It is true indeed, that from the reign of *Edward* III. or however from the time that the ufage of annual Parliaments ceafed, to about the middle of this century (when a motion was made in the year 1744, for *annual* Parliaments, and loft but by thirty-two) the nation feems never to have nurtured the idea of giving Parliament a fhorter continuance than for three years. To what this can be owing, is not eafy to fay. It feems as if one or other of the above interpretations given to the ftatutes of *Edward* III. preponderated in fome meafure over the refiftance of the people, or at leaft over their wifh to refift farther than the terms on which their exertions were made.

the feptennal act the feft violaof Law, ftitution, Decency.

But if thofe interpretations led to the triennial acts above-mentioned, as the beft compromife that could be taken with any proper care of the interefts of the people, they laid they foundation, or the pretence at leaft, for another act in a fubfequent period, which was by no means fo innocent and moderate as the triennial fcheme, was neither fought nor approved by the people, nor had any one principle to ftand on, that bore the leaft approximation either to conftitutional ideas, or to any fenfible ftable policy. To the firft indeed it made no pretenfion, but on the contrary affumed a degree of apology for departing from thence, on the fcore of temporary expedience; while there is an infidioufnefs couched under the fcope of it, which would hinder it's own apology from binding too far, and derange at once all conftitutional notions, by eftablifhing the precedent of altering the duration of Parliament at pleafure. I mean here the *Septennial Act*, paffed in the firft year of *George* I. If the
interpretations

interpretations of *Edward's* statutes introduced a latitude into the continuance of Parliament beyond a year, this act carried that latitude beyond all bounds. It was, in short, a palpable and bold violation both of *Law* and *Constitution*. Of *Law*, because the *Triennial* Act under *William* III. having ordained that " from thenceforth no " Parliament whatsoever, that should at any time there- " after be called, assembled, or held, should have any " continuance longer than for three years only at the " farthest," and thus having drawn the line *ultra qua non*, became in this circumstance a sort of *Magna Charta*, sacred in it's obligation, on the faith of which the Country rested. *Of the Constitution*, because whether Parliaments were *annual* or not in their fundamental institution, they were *frequent* ; in this view there is no more affinity in a septennial bill to ancient usage, than it can have to any wise Constitution for giving security and force to the elective rights of a people. The pretence would be an insult on common sense. Nor did that act infringe less upon *Decency* than on *Law* and *Constitution*. For, under the advantage of present possession, it stole from the People what they had never given, and what they loudly protested against giving ; it stole an extension of trust, with no better principle than He shews, who should hold over a term which had never been granted him ; or he, who having made his way into a House, by dint of strength carries off whatsoever he shall lift ; or He, who having way-laid another, makes him captive by force, and dooms him to a deprivation of freedom at his own pleasure.

Under this act more ruinous to the virtue of the elec- tors, to the fortunes of the elected, and to the liberties of the whole Country in the space of seventy years, than ever was experienced in any length of time before it,

even

even including the reign of *Charles* II. fo wafteful to liberty, it is our punifhment ftill to abide. Whenever a

at act muft at events be done away.

propitious hour fhall give any degree of reform to the Reprefentation of the Country, this act muft be done away in the firft inftance. No unprejudiced mind can look on it a moment, and patronize it's exiftence. It cannot ftand with any idea of reform. It is incompatible with any degree of efficiency to the elective Rights of a people. It is infufferable in it's whole complexion. At this hour the pretence on which it rofe is gone. And there cannot be an apology in its favor.

w far further muft go.

That act annihilated, there is a degree of policy, as well as of right, left in the queftion, how far further we muft go.

In difcuffing the rights of a People, and projecting their deliverance from wrongs, it is of moment to confult what appears, on the whole view of things before us in the moment, moft practicable in it's meafure, as well as that which is moft ftrictly due in it's extent. In addition to what has been already remarked, concerning the conduct of our forefathers from the difcontinuance of annual Parliaments to the obtaining of the laft triennial Act, there are confiderations arifing from the difference of prefent and ancient times, to which our attention ought not to be fhut. We may revere the conftitutional principle, and be zealous to preferve it: but certainly it is no forfeiture of wifdom to preferve it *as nearly as we can,* all things confidered.

Bifhop *Burnet* fays*, *Anciently, confidering the hafte and hurry in which Parliaments fat, an annual Parliament*

* Burnet's own *Time,* vol. 3. p. 146.

might

might be no great inconvenience to the nation. 'Tis true, their bufinefs was foon finifhed. But they had little to do, It was a good while before the Commons were legifla-tors [+]. They always **carried the purfe**; and in the dif-pofal of that, the vote was very fummary, becaufe the exigencies of the **Government were not** then very mul-tifarious. *Burnet* goes on, *but by reafon of the flow me-thods of Seffions now, an annual Parliament would become a very unfupportable grievance.* 'Tis true the nature of parliamentary bufinefs, and the duration of feffions, **have** changed exceedingly with the multiplicity of our **affairs.** **The** difputed returns of elections have alfo contributed not a little to lengthen out the feffions. And though thefe occafions of delay to the public bufinefs would **pro-**bably be much obviated by fhort Parliaments, and by **the** fhorteft moft of **all :** Though, befides, a very effectual provifion for obviating them has been propofed **in a Bill** already tendered by a noble Duke [*], whofe **difinterefted** **zeal** to ferve his country in this **and every** other impor-tant circumftance will make his name **as** dear to pofterity, as it is revered and confided in by **the** prefent age : yet there would remain, after all, an accumulation of bufi-nefs, flowing in from the infinite occafions of legiflation within the realm, and from **our** dependencies without it, certainly beyond what could ever fill **the** attention of ancient Parliaments under annual elections, perhaps greater than could be difpatched by any feffional Parliament with permanent effect and a comprehenfive policy. Re-flecting on this confideration, **we** may poffibly fee a reafon which, in the increafing progrefs of parliamen-tary bufinefs, might induce **our** forefathers to be fo filent,

[+] Hume's Hift. Engl. v. 2. p. 284 Edit. I.
[*] The Duke of Richmond.

as we have remarked they were for a long period, on annual Parliaments, and to embrace the triennial. And this appears more forcible in refpect to the act obtained under the *firſt Charles*, becauſe it was the firſt, and becauſe *Charles*'s Parliament could not be fuſpected, in that hour of it's maſtery over their Prince, of any exceſſive nicety towards him, or any diſinclination to tie up his hands in the tighteſt manner.

It muſt be confeſſed that the only ground given for a preference of triennial to annual Parliaments, ariſes from the preſent nature of parliamentary buſineſs. In the point of giving the beſt effect to the People's controul over their own delegation, moſt certainly that limitation which brings the delegated truſt back to them moſt ſpeedily, is the ſafeſt from abuſe. But let us beſtow a moment's thought, whether a triennial Parliament is incapable of giving this ſafety in a good degree.

The object to be ſecured is, an impreſſed remembrance on the mind of the repreſentative, that he is the Deputy of others, dependent on their favor for the truſt committed to him, and accountable to them for it. Nothing, to be ſure, can give the hope of effecting this, but making his commiſſion a ſhort one. How then may we count upon the probable feelings of a man, under triennial Parliaments, who has any ſenſe at all of preſerving the favor of his Conſtituents, and eſpecially in ſuch a reformed Repreſentation as ſends him to Parliament from an extenſive community? The firſt winter he takes his ſeat, he comes, if ever, with gratitude on his mind, and a full purpoſe to make good the profeſſion, he has pledged. Inſtances of a Solicitor General giving his very firſt vote contrary to all the expectations of his friends, and Conſtituents are, for the honor of human nature, very rare; and are no more to be taken as arguments that the reft of mankind are likely to act in the fame manner, than it would be fair to deny common fenfe to our fpecies, becaufe fome are ideots, or comelinefs to the human frame, becaufe fome are monfters. If then the love of his Conftituents keeps him honeft the firft winter, the fear of them will do the fame thing in the third and laft. We want no evidence now, even after all the immerfion of five years in corruption, how much the fixth fhall put the worft Parliament on it's guard, and bring forward, in the fupport of fome refolve flattering to the People, names which have all along been regardlefs of all that the Country could fay to them. Thus compreffed between a flow of gratitude on the one hand, and a fear of lofing his re-election on the other, it is not perhaps too credulous to conclude, that a Reprefentative, depending on a popular election, will not venture in the intermediate year to take any meafures, which are daringly contrary to what he knows to be the fenfe of his Electors. At leaft, he muft be caft in a peculiar mould of confidence, if he fhould.

For my own part, I am free to confefs, that under a Reprefentation, though not perfectly, yet confiderably, equalized, I cannot fee danger nor even infecurity in a triennial Parliament; I cannot fee the difference between that and an annual one of very great importance. Perhaps under fuch a reform it were beft, on the whole, to take the former, at leaft for a trial. But were the Reprefentation to continue as it is, the only *fuccedaneum* for it's reform (and a poor one at beft) the only chance to the people not only of maintaining any degree of their refpect

in

in the State, but of efcaping the final ruin of their liberties, is in an annual Parliament.

thout fhort
liaments no
endment of
Reprefenta-
a can do
d.

Frequency of election is the *fine qua non* of our political Rights and our political wifdom. I muft repeat it
again, that without this no poffible amendment of the
Reprefentation can do us good. It is not the choice of
the people that can enfure any thing. Let us fuppofe the
Country ever fo cautious in the men they elect, yet they
cannot change the courfe of human nature, they can neither diveft temptation of it's lure, nor the fwerving heart
of it's aptitude to embrace it. They may fend, perhaps,
their Reprefentative pure from their hands, but in a truft
extended for feveral years their hold over his virtue de-
creafes every day; temptation is invited; the facrifice
is in his own hands; and fhould he think fit to make it,
it is but an empty confolation that they have to pafs their
choice anew in all the amplitude of freedom, when both
prevention and remedy are come too late. But it is fuppofing more, perhaps, than we can ever be warranted to
do in moft popular elections, that warinefs and an attention to the public virtue of the Candidate decide the
choice. The iffue therefore of our liberties and all our
happinefs muft not be left to our weaknefs, any more than
to the chance of his virtue, without a timely remedy;
that if we have been indifcreet, or have placed an im-
proper confidence, his unfitnefs or his want of integrity
may not have the advantage, but may refcue, by the fpeedy
facrifice of it's own fituation, the more precious interefts
of a whole country.

The principle I have laft infifted on is incontrovertible
in the foundeft policy and in all experience; and laughs
at the little objections refpecting repeated expence and repeated

peated tumult. Thofe evils arife from Candidates themfelves, and it would be hard that the People fhould lofe
their rights for mifchiefs created by others, and which
poffibly the enemies of popular freedom might purpofely
create. Or fuppofing thefe inevitable, is there no other
policy than to deprive a whole country of it's rights for
accidental inconveniencies? They fhould be rendered
difficult to be practifed, and perilous to thofe that practife
them. If former laws have failed in thefe effects, the argument from the want of them is now annihilated, to
every man's mind who is not determined to facrifice the
purity of election to fome worfe confiderations, by the
excellent provifions of a Bill propofed laft year by a noble
Lord* already mentioned; which is fo exprefsly calcu-
lated to obviate both the evils above-mentioned in every
degree, that, abftracted from the public good of it, it
fhould feem wonderful how it could meet a difficulty
of reception in that Houfe, whofe fortunes it was calcu-
lated, in the firft inftance, to preferve.

It is poffible, that in fome remarks which have fallen
from me in this chapter, I may not have correfponded
exactly with thofe ideas on the limitation of Parliament,
which have been entertained by many fenfible and worthy
friends of the People, any more than in other parts
of this treatife I have favoured the opinions of thofe,
whom I do not think friendly to the Rights of the Country. But if I have written for no Party (fhould the
friends of the People be called a Party) I have the better
claim to what meets very much the feelings of my own
mind, an independence of fentiment; and I have only
the errors of my judgment to anfwer for. My own heart

* Lord Mahon.

tells me, that the establishment of what is *true* and *right* in the important questions before me is my only object. And if my views shall have succeeded at all in diffusing persuasion through all classes of public characters, and gaining from thence a more general support of a better Representation and Duration of Parliament, I shall think it sufficient, as a citizen, that I have lived for this ; though, as a private man, I may have displeased many. He that writes to please a *Party* will do no good to his Country ; nor let him ever think of doing good to himself, unless he will bring his mind to become a pander to party views. The wonted effects of engaging habits, the finest feelings of the mind, lose their force here, and become extinguished in the prevalence of a coarser and meaner influence. The attention, the attachment, the friendship, the love, which in all other parts of life beget their like, are brushed away by any departure from the narrowness of a selfish system ; and after the expenditure of a long course of years, will not secure the individual from unkindness at the last.

FINIS.

www.ingramcontent.com/pod-product-compliance
Lightning Source LLC
Chambersburg PA
CBHW030629270326
41927CB00007B/1371

* 9 7 8 3 3 3 7 0 6 4 7 1 6 *